ANTHROPOLOGICAL PAPERS

MUSEUM OF ANTHROPOLOGY, UNIVERSITY OF MICHIGAN

No. 6

THE PRECERAMIC HORIZONS OF NORTHEASTERN OKLAHOMA

by

DAVID ALBERT BAERREIS

ANN ARBOR

UNIVERSITY OF MICHIGAN PRESS, 1951

ISBN (print): 978-1-949098-37-2
ISBN (ebook): 978-1-951519-61-2

Browse all of our books at
sites.lsa.umich.edu/archaeology-books.

Order our books from the University of Michigan Press at www.press.umich.edu.

For permissions, questions, or manuscript queries, contact Museum publications by email at umma-pubs@umich.edu or visit the Museum website at lsa.umich.edu/ummaa.

CONTENTS

FIGURES

Page

MAPS

THE PRECERAMIC HORIZONS OF NORTHEASTERN OKLAHOMA[1]

INTRODUCTION

The Ozark region of southwestern Missouri, northwestern Arkansas, and eastern Oklahoma, from an archaeological viewpoint, appears to have been neither a center of high cultural development nor an area of great aboriginal-population density. The basic geological structure of the area, a dissected limestone plateau, is readily dissolved, however, by percolating ground water to form many caves and overhanging bluffs seemingly suitable for Indian habitation. Consequently, when in the early twentieth century American archaeologists first began cave hunting in an attempt to find remains comparable in antiquity to the paleolithic cultures of Europe, the Ozark region became one of the major centers of activity. The great interest in seeking paleolithic remains, which was current in this period, was often unacknowledged. This may perhaps be traced to a marked bias on a large part of the staff of the Smithsonian Institution and Bureau of American Ethnology, a staff including such men as Powell, McGee, Thomas, Holmes, and Hrdlicka, against the assignment of any great antiquity to remains of the American Indian. Nevertheless, the manner in which the work of the archaeologists exploring the Ozark region is reported often reveals this interest in paleolithic material. Peabody and Moorehead (1904), for example, in their description of the excavations conducted in Jacobs Cavern, Missouri, during 1903, prefaced their report with an account of cave exploration in general. In this introduction they stressed the stratigraphic results of work in European caves which yielded evidence of paleolithic man, implying that similar results are to be expected in the New World.

---

[1]Submitted in partial fulfillment of the requirements for the degree of Doctor of Philosophy in the Faculty of Political Science, Columbia University.

While a desire to prove that the Smithsonian experts were mistaken probably stimulated a considerable amount of exploration and excavation, it also led to some slighting of the remains recovered. Where the remains were obviously of no great antiquity, little attention was paid to them. Even when the deposit was of considerable thickness, apparently few attempts were made to determine what cultural changes occurred in the more recent period. Material reported as recently as the explorations of Gerard Fowke (1922) in the Ozark region of Central Missouri shows such an orientation. In the Sell Cave, located one-half mile south of Waynesville, artifacts were obtained in a talus layer having a maximum thickness of six feet. The small series of artifacts described is presented without reference to any possible temporal change. Furthermore, a second stratum six feet in thickness was present below the talus zone and as described was clearly laid down by flowing water. This zone was completely excavated at the expense of five weeks' work though not a single artifact or bone was recovered (Fowke, 1922:45-51). It would seem that an adequate test section could have been carried to bed rock, making the more extensive work unnecessary. The absorbing desire to find early remains blinded some of the first workers to the actual potentialities of their own discoveries.

Though the early explorations of the Ozark region revealed no conclusive evidence of very ancient occupation, new interest in the area was stimulated by the investigations of M. R. Harrington (1924) in bluff shelters on the upper White River in Arkansas and in McDonald County, Missouri, along the Cowskin, or Elk, River. Though the sites were not demonstrably of great antiquity, many contained large quantities of perishable items, such as plant remains, basketry, dressed skin, and textiles, that provided a full account of the mode of life of the occupants of the bluff shelters. Basketry and textile remains had been reported earlier, for example by D. I. Bushnell, Jr. (1915), but not in the richness of these discoveries. A further point of considerable interest was the evidence that the preceramic bluff dwellers not only hunted wild game and gathered wild seeds, but that they were a horticultural people, raising maize, squash, beans, gourds, and the domestic sunflower. Subsequently, additional remains in an equally fine state of preservation were obtained and reported, largely without detail, by S. C. Dellinger at the Conference on Southern Pre-History held at Birmingham, Alabama, in 1932.

Since only preliminary reports have appeared, additional information is urgently needed on this horizon which was horticultural but nonceramic. The Ozark Bluff-Dweller culture, as most of the sites are classified, is inadequately defined, and its chronological position is uncertain. In the description of it little attempt has been made to determine whether all of the materials considered actually constitute a single complex, or to ascertain whether or not various temporal periods are represented. Stone implements have been largely neglected, though any broad comparisons independent of the vagaries of local conditions of preservation must essentially be based upon this cultural category. A suggestion of temporal depth in the region has recently been given by the postulation of a "Proto-Bluff Dweller Culture" (Martin, Quimby, and Collier, 1947:338-39). Though one might intuitively suspect that the agricultural corn-raising Ozark Bluff-Dweller culture is not the only preceramic culture in this area and that some remains of purely hunting groups are present, the summary description of the Proto-Bluff Dweller culture does not establish its presence. The description is given in such general terms that it might well apply to any hunting complex, but it seems to be based largely on the remains at Jacobs Cavern (Peabody and Moorehead, 1904), concerning which Harrington (1924:13) has commented that it "yielded typical Bluff-dweller stonework." A question might therefore be raised as to whether the presence of an earlier culture has been demonstrated.

The general cultural relationships of the preceramic material of the Ozark plateau also need clarification. In his original description of the Ozark Bluff-Dweller culture, Harrington (1924:14-15) listed nineteen typical "characteristics," of which eleven, according to his analysis, pointed toward the Southwest. Harrington, however, was duly cautious of interpreting this as an indication of southwestern origin since he considered it probable that in the past many of these traits had a much wider distribution. Prior to this report, Bushnell (1915:319-20) had described an Ozark coiled basket as a possible trade item from the Southwest. The suggestion of southwestern affiliations, however, has been perpetuated in more recent publications. Wedel (1940:304) has stated that if the antiquity of the Basket-Maker remains occurring in the Oklahoma Panhandle is substantiated and if these remains are shown to be related to the Ozark Bluff-Dweller culture, they may be regarded as local manifestations of an old "Basket

Maker-like" horizon. Martin, Quimby, and Collier (1947: 221,337,342) also referred to a "Basket Maker-like" culture in connection with the complex, stating that there may be such a culture, very broadly defined, that was widespread in North America.

The major problems concerning this period in the Ozark region are clear. Preceramic remains are present that are considered to represent a long period of time. Within such a lengthy period we should expect developmental stages. The published data, however, are not only inadequate for the establishment of such stages, but the cultures themselves are not well defined since the available descriptive accounts stress perishable items and lack essential detail. Relationships with other areas have been suggested and a general Basket-Maker horizon has been postulated, but, again, since in description stress has been placed on perishable items, the degree of relationship may have been influenced in favor of regions in which similar perishable items are present.

A partial solution to many of these problems may be achieved through sites in northeastern Oklahoma on the western periphery of the Ozark Plateau. From 1937 to 1940, prior to the inundation of much of the river valley land by the construction of the Grand River Dam, intensive excavations were conducted in Delaware County. The construction of this dam threatened to impound water that would cover the major archaeological sites of the region, an area for which little information regarding its prehistory was available. Fortunately, at this time the University of Oklahoma was sponsoring a Work Projects Administration archaeological program, directed by Dr. Forrest E. Clements, then of the Department of Anthropology of that university. By expanding this work in Delaware County it was possible to conduct excavations at the important sites that were to be flooded, though there was considerable pressure of time because of the scope of the work. Many of these sites revealed evidence of an extensive early occupation, since pottery was lacking or confined to the uppermost part of the bluff-shelter and midden deposits. The superposition of Hopewellian and other Woodland pottery types on these deposits would give, according to present estimates, an approximate terminal date to the preceramic occupation of not later than A.D. 900-1200. The exposed nature of the sites, for the deposits were not protected from rainfall, resulted in the recovery of only nonperishable artifacts of stone or, rarely, of bone. Consequently, it is possible to describe only a small part of the total culture complex. The account we can give for this culture complex is strikingly different from that usually given for the Ozark Bluff-Dweller culture, in which the stress is often placed on perishable items of the culture. We are nevertheless able to make some valid comparisons with the Bluff-Dweller culture, on the basis of the few stone implements that have been described, and also to make broader comparisons on the basis of the total complex of stone implements as revealed by the Oklahoma components.

Three of the sites excavated for the University of Oklahoma in the Grand River Dam area have been selected for description and analysis in Section I. On the basis of the materials at these sites, three sequent periods may be defined. The general absence of large milling stones in the first of these periods suggests a stage in which hunting was far more important in the economy than the gathering of wild seeds. In the two following periods the abundance of large milling stones indicates the growing importance of seed gathering and presumably of agriculture, though the horizon was still preceramic. This change in economy and the similarity of stone-artifact types to many types reported for the Ozark Bluff-Dweller culture, suggest that the last two periods, defined on the basis of the material found in the Oklahoma components, represent the same complex as the Ozark Bluff-Dweller culture. A comparative survey of preceramic horizons in the Southeast and Southwest indicates a marked similarity in forms. The general absence, however, of elaborated forms in bone and ground or polished stone which are typical of the eastern Archaic raises a problem as to the relationship with this complex, the solution of which may rest upon our attaining an understanding of the stages of development of the Archaic or, alternatively, the Ozark complex may be explained as a peripheral variant or even a late attenuated survival. It would appear that certain general similarities, which have been stressed previously in many sites remote from one another, can be explained on other grounds than the possession of a common cultural base which implies the spread of a single culture. Not only is a strong possibility of the derivation of similar elements from diverse sources to be considered, but there may also be a convergence due to a similar functional situation. Both the

Southwest and the Ozark region passed from a hunting, or hunting and gathering stage, to one where the stress was on the utilization of seeds obtained either through gathering or horticulture. This intensive utilization of seeds at a time when pottery was not manufactured in either area might well lead to similar but independent elaborations in basketry, one of the main items of material culture on which relationships between the two regions have been postulated.

The general organization of material in the succeeding sections is as follows. Section I deals with the description of the locations and an analysis of artifactual material from three sites in Delaware County, northeastern Oklahoma: the Evans Midden site (DlEvIII), the Caudill site (DlCaI), and the McConkey site (DlMcVII). An attempt has been made here to conserve space and to give a narrative treatment regarding the general nature of the cultural materials. A more detailed, tabular analysis suitable for further comparative studies is presented as Appendix I. The typological categories utilized in the description of projectile-point types and scrapers have been defined on the basis of a much larger series from this region. A marked feature of the area is the persistence of similar forms from very early horizons through late ones. The typological categories, therefore, are sufficiently broad to accommodate the minor changes in form which occurred during this span of time. This does not indicate that the projectile points, for instance, in all these horizons are identical. They vary in size and proportions and in the relative frequency of such component features as shape of base and blade. The frequency of these component features is given in Appendix I, and supplemental details of size and proportion in Appendix II. Section II is a comparative analysis of the Oklahoma components in which the sequent stages of the preceramic horizon of northeastern Oklahoma are defined. Section III is comparative: first, the stages of northeastern Oklahoma are compared and equated with other sites and cultures in the general Ozark Plateau area, and, second, the general relationship of these stages to other preceramic horizons in both the East and Southwest is considered. Section IV presents the general conclusions which may be drawn from this study.

ACKNOWLEDGMENTS

The archaeologist, perhaps more than anyone else, draws heavily upon the work of his predecessors and contemporaries. Any published report of archaeological field work in many untold ways reflects co-operation and assistance at all stages. Locating sites and obtaining permission to dig require assistance of the type generously given by Mr. Alfred Reed, of Grove, Oklahoma. The successful continuation of an excavation program requires direction, such as that given in this instance by Dr. Forrest E. Clements. Later, when the collections are studied, one must have the co-operation of the officials in charge of the materials. This was obtained from Dr. J. Willis Stovall, of the University Museum, Norman, Oklahoma, and from Dr. Robert E. Bell, of the Department of Anthropology of the University of Oklahoma. Among many whose suggestions have improved the text are Dr. William Duncan Strong and Dr. Julian Steward. The whole process from excavation to publication is an encouraging example of the type of co-operation which is possible in a world that at times appears to lack the spirit of mutual helpfulness. If a full list of names were given rather than this very brief acknowledgment, doubts about the possibility of co-operation among men would soon be resolved.

I. PRECERAMIC SITES IN NORTHEASTERN OKLAHOMA

A. THE EVANS MIDDEN SITE - DlEvIII. (Location: NE. 1/4 NE. 1/4 SW. 1/4 sec. 22, T. 24 N., R. 23 E.)

Earth containing artifacts and other evidence of human occupation attained a thickness of 15 feet in parts of this midden, far exceeding in this aspect any other site in Delaware County. The site is located at the west side of the mouth of a narrow valley. The valley, known locally as Woodward Hollow, contains a small intermittent stream, fed by a series of small springs, which empties near the site into Grand River. At this point Grand River makes a wide bend cutting against the rolling limestone hills. Because of this cutting action the broad terraces on the north side of the river are compressed into two narrow terraces, on the uppermost of which the site is located. In the small subsidiary valley a sloping hillside continues to rise several hundred yards back of the flat terrace. Erosion from this hillside could have contributed in part to the formation of the deposit so that thickness alone is not convincing evidence of any considerable antiquity. The general location of this and the other sites described is indicated on the map of the Grand River lake area (Map 1).

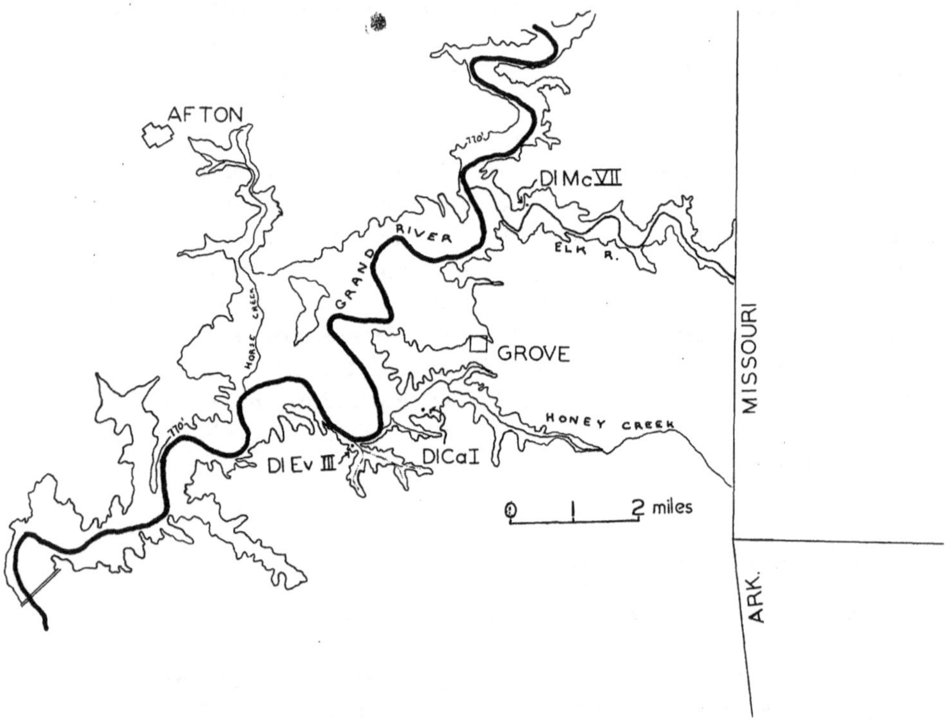

Map. 1. The Grand River Lake Area in Northeastern Oklahoma.

After the productive areas of the midden were located by tests, the site was covered by a grid of 10-foot squares. Further testing and excavation indicated that marked soil changes and distinct strata were lacking in the deposit. Approximately the upper 4 feet were stained black by humus material; below this point the soil changed gradually to a chocolate-colored loam.

In the absence of natural soil lines that could be followed in the excavation, the deposit was removed in horizontal 4-inch levels. Excavations at this site were conducted after water had already begun to be impounded by the dam, earlier work having been concentrated on sites at lower contour levels. Since the full depth of the site had not been appreciated at the time early tests were made, only a limited section of the very deep deposits could be excavated before the rising water flooded the lowest section of the excavations. A single row of 10-foot squares running north and south through the deposit was excavated to the base of the earth containing culture remains. The materials described in detail from DlEvIII in this report are confined to the preceramic parts of the row of squares excavated to the base of the midden.

Pottery was present only in the upper part of the midden and even there was not abundant since only 381 sherds were recovered. Ninety-six per cent of the sherds were confined to the upper two feet; only 10 sherds were found at deeper levels ranging from 24 to 60 inches. Since 6 of the 10 sherds were in the 24- to 28-inch level and the remaining 4 were widely scattered in the lower part of the deposit, it seems reasonable to assume that they may have owed their deeper position at the time of excavation to rodent action. It was not possible, however, to trace any definite rodent holes in the area in which they occurred. Their position was largely concentrated in the western part of the area excavated, some 90 feet from the trench penetrating to the deeper levels, so that the problem of their deeper occurrence does not immediately enter into the discussion of the material considered here. The very deep sherds were typologically similar to those of shallower levels, which adds further support to the possibility of rodent action. The pottery as a whole is from two distinct culture complexes. The upper 8 inches contained a shell-tempered variety, Neosho Punctated, which is attributed to the Neosho Focus, an Upper Mississippi complex (Baerreis, 1939:3; 1940). Below this was found grit-tempered pottery of a Hopewellian type.

Since we are here concerned with the preceramic cultures of northeastern Oklahoma, in the light of the vertical distribution of pottery, only artifacts at a depth of 32 inches and below in squares 1:3 through 6:3 are considered in this report (see Map 2, p. 98). Even with this elimination of nearly the top 3 feet of the deposit, we deal here with a cultural zone 12 feet in thickness.

Since this should give an excellent opportunity to observe temporal changes in the preceramic complex, the initial analysis of artifacts was made in terms of the level in which they occurred. The top of the deposit across the 60-foot section under consideration had only a slight curvature. Levels representing the same depth from the surface were combined, though we have no actual proof that a horizontal deposition of material continued throughout the occupation of the site. This was suggested, however, by a similar horizontal frequency of artifacts throughout this section of the deposit. A study by individual squares revealed few significant differences among the separate columns, those present possibly being due to the size of the sample.

Artifacts were not abundant in the deep levels though they occurred in considerable variety. The presence of scrapers, small grinding stones, abraders, knives, and drills, in addition to projectile points, suggests that this was not a hunting station at which only a limited range of artifacts would be expected because of the temporary nature of the occupation. It indicates, rather, that this was a site at which peoples camped either continuously or sporadically, and one where all the economic activities of the community were carried on. Zones in which fragments of charcoal became more abundant were encountered, but there appeared to be no specially prepared fireplaces. No burials could be definitely attributed to the preceramic levels, although they were present in the upper part of the deposit. Cache pits and indications of house structures were also lacking.

Table I presents the vertical distribution of all artifacts found below 32 inches in the six squares selected for analysis. In the table the artifacts are broken down into categories to show the nature of the cultural materials, but we may largely ignore the individual categories to consider the totals in the last column in regard to the intensity of occupation during the gradual accumulation of the deposit. The frequency of specimens clearly indicates that there were two major periods of intensive occupation of the site. The more recent of these fell in the uppermost part of the section of the deposit described. It was preceded by a period of approximately equal length of time, to judge by the thickness of the deposit, during which specimens indicating human occupation were much less abundant. In turn, this was preceded by another period of intensive occupation, and then in the deepest part of the deposit artifacts were again rather scarce. The rhythmical nature of the changes

TABLE I

Frequency of Specimens in Arbitrary Four-Inch Levels, Site DlEvIII

Number	Four-inch Levels	Projectile Points	Bunts	Stemmed Scrapers	Other Scrapers	Drills	Knives	Core Knives	Choppers	Fragments	Cores	Flakes	Small Grinding Stones	Abraders	Large Grinding Stones	Anvils, Hammerstones	Miscellaneous	Total
9	32-36	25	..	..	1	1	1	2	3	16	19	7	..	1	2	..	1	79
10	36-40	22	..	..	1	..	9	4	5	24	19	10	2	..	1	..	..	97
11	40-44	15	..	..	..	..	7	2	4	33	15	1	..	1	..	..	..	78
12	44-48	12	..	..	2	..	7	8	2	35	10	8	1	..	1	1	..	87
13	48-52	6	1	..	..	..	2	2	1	14	2	5	1	..	..	..	..	34
14	52-56	6	..	..	..	..	2	1	..	7	3	2	..	..	..	..	..	21
15	56-60	4	..	..	1	..	2	..	..	6	1	2	..	1	1	..	..	18
16	60-64	4	..	..	..	..	..	..	1	4	3	1	..	..	..	..	..	13
17	64-68	..	..	..	..	..	..	..	2	3	..	1	..	..	..	..	..	6
18	68-72	1	..	..	..	..	..	..	..	2	2	..	..	..	..	..	..	5
19	72-76	3	..	..	1	..	..	1	1	1	2	..	..	..	..	..	..	9
20	76-80	1	..	..	..	..	..	..	..	3	..	..	..	..	..	..	..	4
21	80-84	3	..	..	..	..	..	..	..	1	2	1	..	..	..	..	..	7
22	84-88	2	..	..	1	..	..	..	..	2	2	2	..	..	..	..	..	9
23	88-92	1	..	..	1	..	2	..	..	9	..	1	..	..	..	..	..	14
24	92-96	2	..	..	..	..	2	1	1	1	2	..	..	..	..	..	..	9
25	96-100	1	..	..	..	..	..	..	..	..	..	..	..	..	..	..	..	1
26	100-104	3	..	..	..	..	..	..	..	1	3	1	..	..	..	..	..	8
27	104-108	1	..	..	..	..	2	1	..	7	1	..	..	..	..	..	..	12
28	108-112	5	1	1	1	..	1	..	..	7	4	1	..	..	..	..	..	21
29	112-116	6	1	..	1	..	4	4	..	11	5	1	..	1	..	..	1	35
30	116-120	13	..	..	2	..	1	4	2	11	..	3	..	1	1	1	..	39
31	120-124	7	..	..	3	1	1	4	2	9	2	1	..	1	..	..	..	31
32	124-128	6	..	..	4	1	1	1	1	7	5	7	3	3	..	..	..	39
33	128-132	2	..	1	..	..	3	..	1	2	4	1	1	1	..	..	..	16
34	132-136	1	..	..	1	..	3	..	..	3	3	..	3	..	..	..	..	14
35	136-140	..	..	..	..	..	1	2	..	2	1	..	..	..	..	..	..	6
36	140-144	2	..	..	..	..	..	1	..	1	..	..	..	..	..	..	..	4
37	144-148	..	..	..	1	..	..	..	..	1	1	..	..	..	..	..	..	3
38	148-152	..	..	..	..	..	..	..	..	3	..	..	..	..	..	..	..	3
39	152-156	1	..	..	..	..	1	..	..	..	..	..	..	..	..	..	..	2
40	156-160	..	..	..	..	..	..	..	..	1	..	..	..	..	..	..	..	1
41	160-164	..	..	..	..	..	1	..	..	2	..	..	..	..	..	..	..	3
42	164-168	..	..	..	..	..	..	..	..	..	..	..	..	..	..	..	..	0
43	168-172	..	..	..	..	..	..	1	..	2	..	..	..	..	..	..	..	3
44	172-176	..	..	..	..	..	..	..	..	1	..	..	..	..	..	..	..	1
45	176-180	..	..	..	..	..	..	..	..	1	..	..	..	..	..	..	..	1

in the deposit suggests something like a seasonal change in occupation but the thickness of each of the sections of deposit involved, ranging from 3 to 4 feet, precludes such an interpretation. It seems more likely that the deposit indicates occupation by a relatively mobile population, large segments of which would move to a different area, possibly because of depletion of the local game supplies, and then return when the former area had become replenished. There appears to be no period during which the site was entirely abandoned for a long time, since no continuous sterile area was to be found. Between the periods of intensive occupation the site must therefore have been inhabited, or at least visited frequently, by small family groups.

The interpretation given above is believed to refer to the intermittent occupation of a single cultural group. The two peaks of occupation could, of course, represent successive occupations by different cultural complexes but, as will be shown in the analysis of artifacts, the cultural inventory for the two peaks is strikingly similar. Nevertheless, these changing periods of intensity of occupation could well reveal phases in the local evolution of culture. While the artifact inventory and description could be given in terms of each arbitrary excavation level, the number of artifacts in each level was so small that it would be difficult to see trends or changes in those levels. Because of the absence of natural stratigraphy, the zones for comparative and sequential study have been selected on the basis of frequency of artifacts. The 4 zones selected correspond to the vertical sections described previously in which the frequency of artifacts differs markedly. The zones are lettered A to D, Zone A being the lowermost level. Zone D consists of the period of most intensive occupation found in the 4-inch levels Nos. 9 to 16, at a depth of from 32 to 64 inches. Zone C is a somewhat thicker section of deposit with less intensive indications of occupation, which is found in the 4-inch levels Nos. 17 to 26, at a depth of from 64 to 104 inches. Zone B is the earlier period of intensive occupation found in the 4-inch levels Nos. 27 to 34, at a depth of from 104 to 136 inches. Zone A is the earliest period of scanty occupational remains represented by 4-inch levels Nos. 35 to 45, at a depth of from 136 to 180 inches. All changes which are noted in artifact types or in the frequency of artifact types are discussed in terms of these major levels.

The artifacts found in the deposit are largely chipped-stone forms, only a small number of ground and polished forms being present. It is, therefore, obvious that chipped-stone implements will best provide the basis of the definition of the complex and will reveal any temporal changes that are present. For this reason it seems necessary to describe the chipped-stone implements in terms of rather precise typological categories. It should be noted, for example, that while in site DlEvIII these types are described on the basis of only a very few specimens in each category, the type itself was defined on the basis of a much larger series of implements from this general area. Where there are but a few projectile points or other implements of an unusual form, which do not conform to the types defined, those implements are not given a typological designation but are retained in a miscellaneous category until their significance can be determined by further investigation. Though current discussion regarding typological procedure has in general been against the designation of types by number or letter, preferring instead a descriptive name (for example, Krieger, 1944), a combination letter and number designation has been utilized in this report. This procedure has been followed because the definition of the types is considered tentative. Since the full range and variation of the type is not known, a final definition will require modification of the type descriptions presented here. Furthermore, the utility of all of the types has not been demonstrated. The naming of types may more properly await a later stage of research on this area and horizon.

The descriptive section of this report, particularly in the discussion of projectile points, does not include a full discussion of the variation in shape of base, body outline, and other component features of the projectile points. The utility of a detailed analysis of these features is not clear at present, but with the increasing availability of additional comparative material, such an analysis may prove of value in the future. The frequency of the various component features is, therefore, given in Appendix I in tabular form as part of a detailed trait list. The frequency of projectile points given in Table I exceeds the number classified into types. The reason for the discrepancy is that the table includes all recognizable projectile points even though their fragmentary condition makes it impossible to classify them as to type.

Work in Chipped Stone

The most abundant form of artifact is the projectile point. All are sufficiently large to be classed as dart points rather than arrow points if we accept the division that is currently made in archaeological literature. This problem of interpretation deserves careful consideration (see Kidder, 1938). The various types recognized for this site and their frequencies are given in Table II. The percentage column gives the per cent of each type among the total points in that zone. On the basis of this table it is obvious that there are not enough classifiable points in Zone A to warrant its segregation from Zone B. The major trends which can be detected in the projectile points, therefore, are those to be seen among zones B, C, and D. Since the total number of projectile points in each zone differs considerably, trends of increasing or decreasing popularity are more readily appreciated in terms of percentages rather than in terms of absolute frequency. The discussion, therefore, revolves around percentages of points in each zone as indicated in the table.

TABLE II

Distribution of Projectile Point Types, Site DlEvIII

Type	Zone A		Zone B		Zone C		Zone D	
	Number	Per cent	Number	Per cent	Number	Per cent	Number	Per cent
A1	..	..	1	2.5	..	..	2	3
A2	..	..	3	8	..	..	2	3
A3	..	..	1	2.5	..	..	..	..
B1	..	..	4	10	1	8	6	9
B2	..	..	3	8	1	8	34	51
B3	..	..	..	..	..	..	3	4.5
C	..	..	1	2.5	..	..	..	..
E1	2	100	24	62	6	50	9	13
E2	..	..	2	5	1	8	11	16
H	..	..	..	..	3	25	1	.5

The various Type A projectile points are present only in zones B and D. These points have a stem which contracts from the point of attachment to the blade toward the base. The stem is formed by removing an asymmetrical area rather than a symmetrical notch from each corner of the base. The category is subdivided into three types based on the nature of the shoulder area. In Type A1 the shoulder area is concave, gradually merging with the contracting stem. The stem, therefore, has a concavo-convex contour. The form of the blade and base is variable.

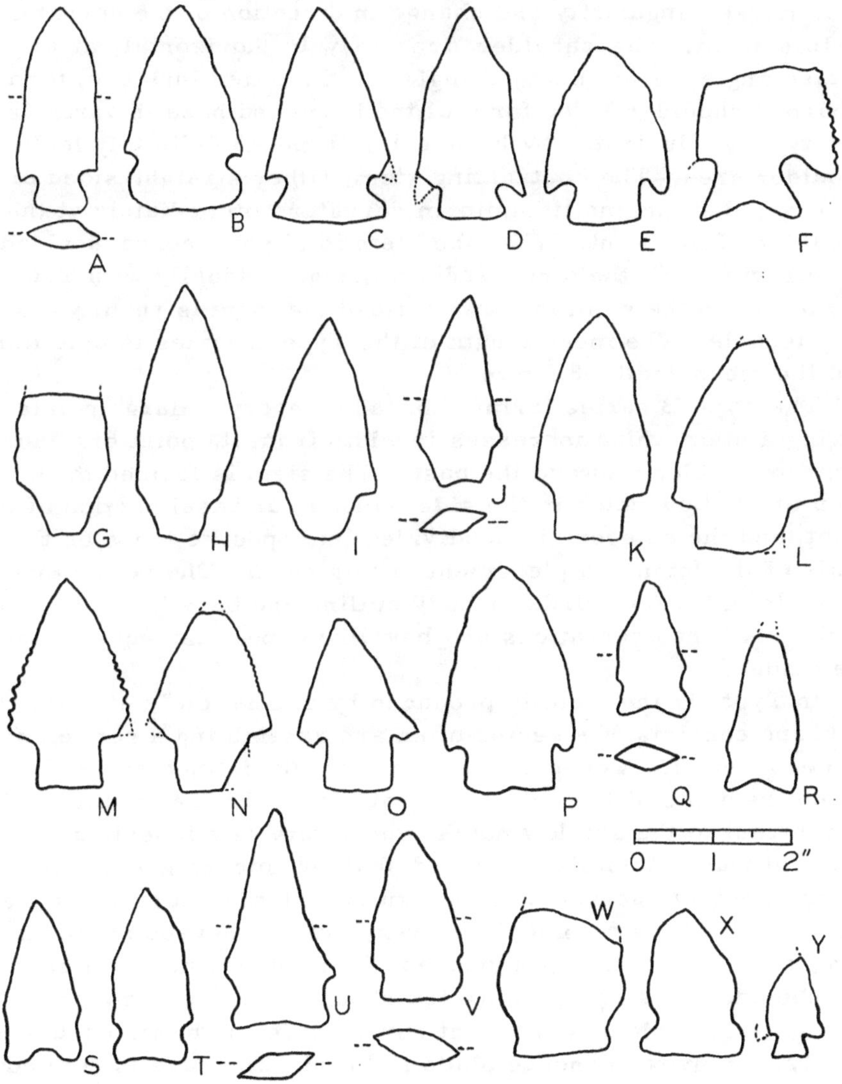

Fig. 1. Projectile Points, Site DlEvIII. A-C — Type B1; D-F — Type B2; G — Type A3; H, J — Type A1; I — Type A2; K-N — Type E1; O, P — Type E2; Q-T — Type H; remainder unclassified. Provenience: Zone D (depth 32-64") — A-E, H-I, O-P, S, V, X-Y; Zone C (depth 64-104") — N, Q-R, T; Zone B (depth 104-136") — F-G, J-M, U, W.

Figure 1H and J illustrates this category with J possessing an alternate bevel on the blade. In Type A2, on the other hand, a distinct shoulder area is present, set off from the stem proper by a marked angularity and change in direction of the curvature at this point. The shoulder area may be horizontal, at an obtuse angle, or at an acute angle; in the latter instance, forming a barbed shoulder. The form of the blade and base is variable. The type is illustrated by Figure 1 I. Type A3 definitely lacks a shoulder area. The contracting stem, either straight sided or convex sided, begins its uniform curvature immediately at the shoulder of the point. When the stem is slightly concave sided, as in Figure 1 G, the form tends to merge gradually with Type A1, but when the stem is convex sided the form is readily distinguishable. The mean length of the Type A series is 85.6 mm. and the mean width 38.0 mm.

The Type B series forms a broad category of large points having a stem which increases in width from its point of attachment to the blade toward the base. The stem is formed by a deep or shallow notch in the side, corner, or basal section of the point, and the category is subdivided into specific types on the basis of the form and placement of this notch. The points are variable in form of blade or body outline and base throughout the series. Coarse serrations and beveling appear infrequently on the blade.

In Type B1 the stem is produced by a "shallow" notch which in shape consists of a sector of an arc resembling a section of a "deep" notch. A deep notch is arbitrarily defined as one in which the depth of the notch is greater than the maximum width, in contrast to the shallow notch, where this relationship does not hold true. Actually, deep and shallow notches grade into each other by minute degrees. The resultant stem is curved and flaring. The blade is commonly convex, with the degree of curvature ranging from slight to pronounced. Maximum width is either at the shoulder or slightly above the shoulder. Less commonly, a straight-sided blade with slight curvature near the tip occurs and, rarely, a convexo-concave blade is found. The base is commonly straight or convex, infrequently concave. Similar variation in blade and base is to be found in the other Type B forms. The type is present in nearly equal quantities in zones B, C, and D. Since the number of points included in the type is small, it is difficult to assess the significance of variation in component features. The type is illustrated by Figure 1 A-C.

Type B2 projectile points have a stem produced by a deep notch, flaked diagonally in each corner. This type shows one of the significant changes in frequency present at the site. In zones B and C it constitutes 8 per cent of the points. In zone D the percentage rises to 51, a frequency more than three times that of any other type in this zone. Some minor variations in form, such as the appearance of a biconcave blade form, in Zone D only, may also be a significant change, though the frequency is not sufficiently large for a conclusive statement. The type is illustrated by Figure 1 D-F.

Type B3 projectile points have a stem which is similarly produced by a deep notch, but the notch is formed in the basal part of the original blank. The notches are more nearly vertical, forming thick, rounded, or squared barbs. The resultant stem is consequently more nearly parallel sided. The type is found only in Zone D, where it constitutes 4.5 per cent of the points.

For the combined Type B series, the mean length is 60.5 mm. and the mean width 37.8 mm. The point illustrated in Figure 1 Y, though fragmentary, is clearly the smallest point present at the site, and comes from Zone D, the most recent zone. A reconstruction of its probable size would give a point somewhat larger than the form classified as Type G3 in other sites, Type G being interpreted as a size probably used with an arrow rather than with a dart.

Type C points have a distinct form and are markedly uniform in their component features. In contrast to the other types which exhibit considerable variation in skill of workmanship and bear crude to exceptional flaking, Type C points are, in general, of exceptional workmanship, exhibiting fine pressure flaking that yields regular, even edges and a symmetrical outline. The blade is consistently convex sided with the maximum width normally located above the shoulder, frequently as much as 15 mm. above that point. The stem has a uniform curvature from the point of attachment to the blade toward the base. The form of the shoulder region is variable, though generally there is a gradual contraction from the shoulder to the point of minimum width of the stem and then a slight flare to the base. Though the expansion to the base is found in all points, this is rather slight and ranges around 2 mm. Because of the curvature in the shoulder region, this sector is difficult to place in categories and varies from a rare barbed form to one roughly horizontal, and most commonly appears as an obtuse form. Bases are either straight or convex. The type is marked by considerable variation in length, but with only a slight range in width, length of stem, and width of base. In general, the points tend to be smaller than those of the Type B series, which are closest to them in form. A common and distinctive feature is a smoothing of the base and sides of the stem through grinding. Though the description of the point may indicate a marked similarity to Type B1, in practice the types are readily distinguished. Type B1 gives the visual impression of being a single geometric form with notches flaked from the corners. In Type C the stem is proportionately small and appears to be a separate area attached to the blade. This type is represented at D1EvIII by a single fragmentary example, which occurred in Zone B.

Type E projectile points consist of a group characterized by a stem which is roughly square or rectanguloid in outline. This feature is present in purity only where a parallel-sided stem is combined with a straight base. The points, however, vary from this ideal standard in having a stem which expands or contracts slightly toward the base. This expansion or contraction of the stem has a straight-sided contour, and not the curved one of types B and C. Where the contraction toward the base is greater than 1 to 2 mm., the point is classified as Type B, but where it is less, the visual appearance is that of a square stem, and the point is retained in Type E. The expanding stem points are retained in this category despite the extent of the expansion, though normally this is not great. From the description given in the preceding pages it would appear that Type E points are similar to those of types A1 or C, both of which differ from it only in having a curved stem. The total appearance of the various types, however, gives the impression that distinct concepts of form are involved.

Type E1 consists of points having a parallel-sided stem, or one with a slight contraction to the base (less than 2 mm.). The points of this type have a mean length of 72.7 mm., a mean width of 38.5 mm., and a mean stem length of 17.8 mm. The type is a dominant one in zones B and C, represented by 62 per cent and 50 per cent of the points, respectively. In Zone D the percentage declines to 13 per cent. Type E2 projectile points, having an expanding rather than a parallel-sided stem, increase in frequency to Zone D. Though not as marked as the trend in Type E1, the transition from 5 to 8 to 16 per cent in zones B, C, and D, respectively, seems important. Type E2 points have a mean length of 61.0 mm., a mean width of 38.0 mm., and a mean stem length of 16.1 mm. Type El is illustrated in Figure 1K-N, Type E2 in Figure 1O-P.

A final category, Type H projectile points, may also appear to be a variant of Type A1, but its features recur consistently and its form has distinctive characteristics so that it deserves separate classification. The stem in this type is formed by flaking a rounded area from the side of the original blank. This is flaked to form a base of approximately the same width as the shoulder. The central part of the base is deeply or slightly concave, with the outer edges curving in the opposite direction to produce a lobed or eared form of stem. The blade is commonly straight sided and frequently bears a bevel on one face, or alternately on both faces. Grinding of the base and/or stem is commonly found on the type. The mean length of points of this type at site D1EvIII is 51.3 mm. and the mean width 25.0 mm. The type appears first in Zone C and comprises 25 per cent of the projectile points. It continues through Zone D, where it is represented by a single point (.5 per cent). Type H is illustrated by Figure 1Q-T.

The additional projectile points, not grouped into types, are most abundant in Zone D, as might be expected since this zone contains the largest number of projectile points. The range in variation in these deviant forms is illustrated in Figure 1U-X. Figure 1U is a distinctive form which appears in Zone B. The point has a concave-sided blade bearing a steeply retouched alternate bevel. A distinct shoulder area is lacking, the stem being concave sided with the narrowest point roughly at the midpoint of the stem length. Figure IV has actually been classified as a Type E2 point, but is segregated in the illustration to indicate that it represents a deviant form that may well warrant separate classification. The stem is proportionately short and there is a tendency toward a convex side. The convex-sided blade has a marked bevel on the edge of one face. This point comes from Zone D. Figure 1W, a point from Zone B, is unusual in being convex at the shoulder region and gradually contracting in width below that point to a juncture with an expanding stem. Figure 1X, the final deviant point in Zone D, is a large point having shallow notches in the side. The general appearance of the point, with the stem wider than the body at the shoulder area, is roughly similar to the small side-notched points in late horizons. In size (length, ca. 50 mm.; width, 33 mm.) it is, of course, unlike these small points.

Other differences which should be stressed in regard to the projectile points of the different zones are the relative frequency of such features as serration, beveling, and the grinding of the base and/or sides of the stem. Large, coarse serrations are an unusual feature for large projectile points, though serrations occur commonly on small projectile points in late horizons. At D1EvIII this feature is present on two points of Type E1, one in Zone B and one in Zone C. It also occurs on a projectile point of Type B2 in Zone B, and is noted on a fragment of the blade of a point found in Zone C. The feature, therefore, occurs on a total of four points distributed only in zones B and C. Considering the small number of projectile points recorded for the site, particularly in the lower zones, the frequency suggests that it is a significant trait for use in the definition of the early complex. Beveling of the blade occurs in several forms. It is found both as a steep alternate bevel on both faces of the blade, and also as a single bevel present on only one face. Like the serrations, this feature is found on projectile points of several different types (Type A1, Type E2, Type H, and as an unclassified point). The distribution of the feature according to zone is as follows: Zone B, 2; Zone C, 1; and Zone D, 1. The beveling, too, seems more characteristic of zones B and C than of the later Zone D. The smoothing of the base and stem through grinding is also a feature which occurs more frequently in the lower zones. The feature is most commonly found in Type E1 points, though it is also present in small quantities in Type A1, Type B2, Type E2, and Type C. The distribution of the feature according to zone is as follows: Zone B, 16; Zone C, 2, and Zone D, 3.

While the outlines of projectile points given in Figure 2 and subsequent figures adequately indicate the shapes of the projectile points, they fail to give any conception of the type of flaking. A representative series of points from the preceramic components is, therefore, given in the form of photographs in Plate I.

One modified projectile-point form found at the site is the bunt. This differs from projectile points in that the end or tip of the blade is intentionally rounded rather than pointed. Two varieties of bunts are distinguished, though one may simply result from usage rather than from a primary difference in function. In one form the blade is rounded and sharp, the edge having been produced by careful pressure flaking from both faces. In the other, the blade is also rounded and is produced in the same manner, but in addition is blunted and battered, with the appearance of having been struck against a hard surface. The first variety suggests the possibility that it may have been hafted and used as a knife, while the second clearly seems to have been a blunt-tipped projectile point. The first variety occurs as a single example in both zones B and D, and the second, the blunt variety, only as a single specimen in Zone B. The bunts are illustrated in Figure 2C-D. They are shown beside the stemmed scrapers (A-B) with which they are often confused. The flaking on the end of the scraper, produced from one face only, and also the frequent presence of a gloss, indicate quite clearly its scraping function.

Chipped-stone drills also occurred only in limited numbers in the deposit, though in varied forms. One specimen (Figure 2K) from Zone D has the appearance of having been derived from a lanceolate-shaped blade. One side is crudely flaked inward to produce a thick, irregular drill shaft though no marks of such usage are present on the specimen. Its dimensions are as follows: length, 79 mm; width, 35 mm.; thickness, 10 mm. The remaining two specimens were recovered in Zone B and show more careful workmanship, particularly in the shaft of the drill. One (Figure 2L) has a roughly rounded base, 44 mm. in width and 45 mm. in height with a thickness of 12 mm. The sides of the base are rather irregular and the flaking bold. The tip of the drill is missing so that it is impossible to determine the maximum length. The other specimen (Figure 2M) bears exceptional flaking and is of a general T-shaped form. The stem has a distinct horizontal shoulder and increases slightly in width to a straight base. The sides and base have been smoothed through grinding. The dimensions of this specimen are as follows: length, 73 mm.; width, 27 mm.; thickness, 7 mm. We may anticipate the conclusions, at this point, to note that in the drills there was a trend of decreasing size toward the more recent periods. It is, therefore, of some value to present the details of size.

Knife forms occur, both as blades having a regular outline produced by careful pressure flaking, and as cruder implements having a more irregular outline, generally a greater thickness,

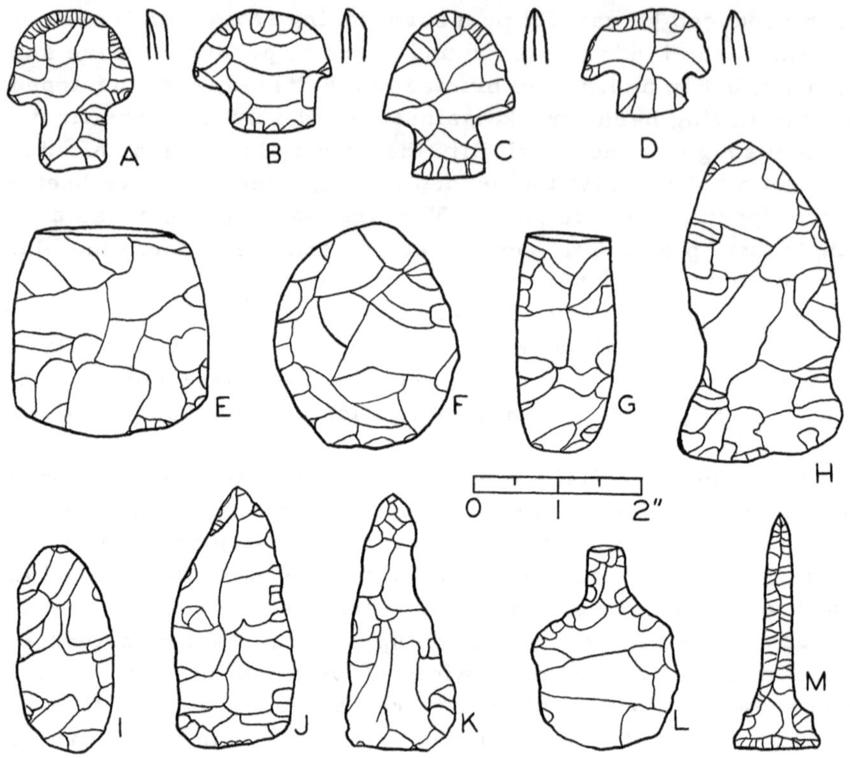

Fig. 2. Chipped Stone Implements, Site DlEvIII. A-B — stemmed scrapers; C-D — bunts; E-J — knives; K-M — drills. Provenience:
Zone D (depth 32-64") — E-F, H, J-K;
Zone C (depth 64-104") — D;
Zone B (depth 104-136") — A-C; I, L-M;
Zone A (depth 136-180") — G.

and a flaking technique that seems to be largely of a percussion type supplemented by some pressure flaking. It is difficult to make a hard and fast division between the two forms since such a division is based in part upon a subjective appraisal, yet the distinction is probably a valid one. The more finished implements are classified as knives, while the second category is designated a core knife.

Only three unbroken knives were collected, all from Zone D.

A general, pointed ovate form is shared by all, one end being pointed while the sides and base are convex. The length ranges from 52 to 99 mm., the maximum width from 35 to 52 mm., and the thickness from 8 to 12 mm. All of the specimens have a biconvex cross section and are carefully flaked on both faces. If the fragmentary specimens are included, it is obvious that this form of implement occurs in all of the zones with no marked differences in size and shape. The major distinction in shape, as far as the entire series is concerned, is between the knives which have a rounded basal zone and those which have a distinct base, usually straight though occasionally slightly convex. The range in maximum width must be extended, on the basis of the fragments, from 30 to 67 mm. The widest specimens occur in Zone D, and narrower lanceolate forms in zones A and B. Core knives appear to have a similar range in shape and size, with the exception of a generally greater thickness. Knife forms are illustrated in Figure 2 E-J.

Scrapers are present in a considerable variety of forms. One distinctive type is the stemmed scraper, representing a modified projectile-point form. While in appearance it has a rounded edge like a bunt, it differs in that the end is flaked from one face only to produce a scraping edge. Both specimens found in the site were in Zone B and have a stem similar to a Type E1 projectile point. The stemmed scraper is shown in Figure 2 A-B. Another scraper form present, which, like the stemmed scraper, is found at different periods of time and in widely separated places, is the side scraper. Scrapers included in this category at D1EvIII are restricted to those forms manufactured from a large primary flake bearing a steep scraper retouch on one or both long edges of the flake. One example was found in Zone C and one in Zone D. A variant specimen included in this type from Zone B has a slight amount of retouching on both faces. Side scrapers are illustrated in Figure 3 K-L.

A large proportion of the remaining scrapers might be considered end scrapers, but grouping in such a large category would not permit the tabulation of the variations in form and technique of manufacture indicated. A series of lettered types is therefore established, based largely on the method by which the scraper was manufactured.

Type B scrapers have a ventral face (the opposite face from the one upon which the scraping edge occurs) which consists of a single flake scar. Many specimens manufactured in this fashion have a butt end which consists of an unmodified striking platform. In those included in Type B, however, there is no indication that the butt end falls at the point where a blow originally removed the flake from the core. On the other hand, they appear to have been manufactured from odd flakes and show a consequent high variability in shape and size. The specimens range from 44 to 88 mm. in length, from 41 to 56 mm. in width, and from 9 to 28 mm. in thickness. A possible indication of the unplanned nature of the form is the fact that many bear an area of cortex on the dorsal surface, revealing the fact that they had been struck from the outer section of a rolled and weathered pebble of chert. Side retouching to modify the form of the scraper is not present. Type B is illustrated in Figure 3 C-E. One scraper, also classified as Type B (Figure 3 F), was manufactured in a similar manner but has a scraping edge on each face.

Type C scrapers, like the preceding group, have a generally plano-convex cross section. The plane surface, however, is not formed by a single flake scar, produced at the time the flake was struck from the original core, but rather by one of two other possible methods. It was formed either by a natural cleavage plane of the chert, in which case the surface usually bears a heavier patination than the subsequent retouching, or it is formed by several primary flakes. The implements in general are flaked by bold percussion flaking, finer retouching appearing only at the scraping edge. They range in length from 54 to 116 mm., in width from 38 to 74 mm., and in thickness from 10 to 38 mm. It was noted that all of the larger forms, of which there are three specimens ranging from 82 to 116 mm. in length, are in Zone B. Two of these large specimens have retouching continuing along one long side of the implement. Quite clearly, the large, crude scrapers are more characteristic of the earlier horizons. No consistent shape is to be noted in the series. Type C scrapers, from D1EvIII, are illustrated in Figure 3 A-B, H-J.

Another group of scrapers, Type E, does not possess a distinct plano-convex cross section but rather has a roughly biconvex section and has one end "turned" or flaked so that, at that point, the implement is roughly plano-convex in section. One specimen is manufactured from a pebble and traces of cortex remain on both faces. The remainder, however, are

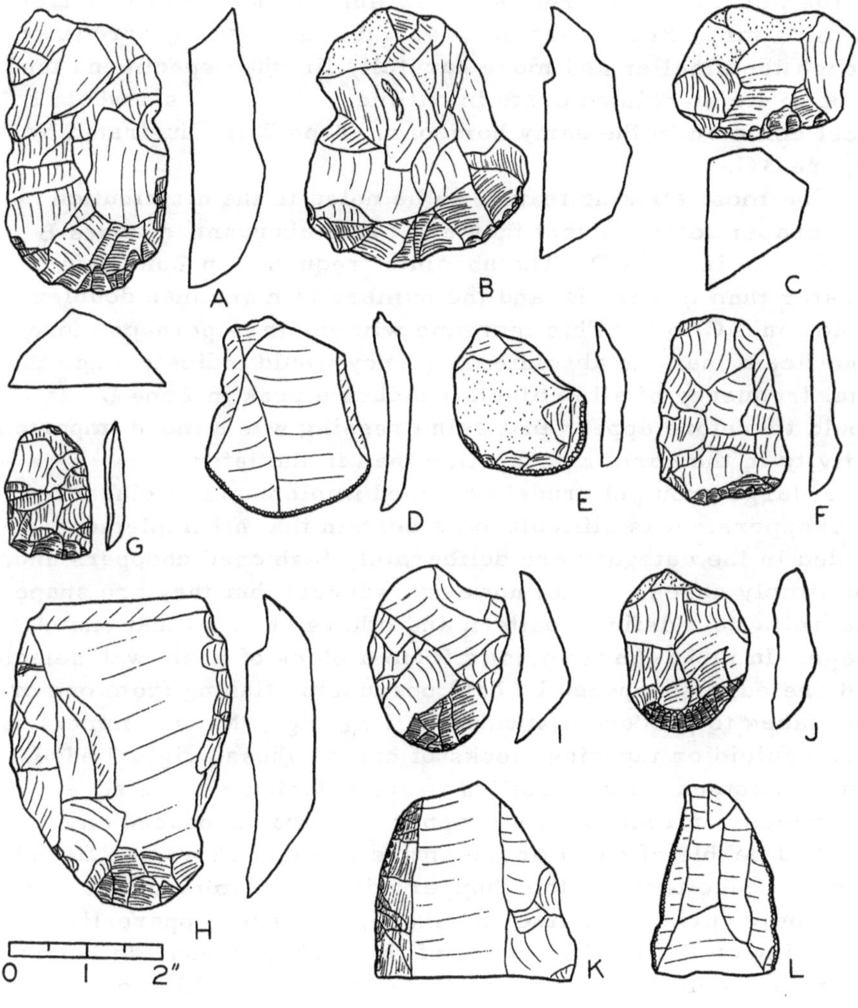

Fig. 3. Scrapers, Site D1EvIII. A-B, H-J — Type C; C-F — Type B; G — Type E; K-L — side scrapers. Provenience:
Zone D (depth 32-64") — G, L;
Zone C (depth 64-104") — C, E;
Zone B (depth 104-136") — A-B, D, F, H-K.

core implements, and both faces have been modified by bold percussion flaking. The implements range in length from 57 to 102 mm., in width from 41 to 75 mm., and in thickness from 11 to 25 mm. Forms are quite variable and usually irregular, though the smaller and more carefully finished specimens tend to be ovate or pointed ovate in outline. The type as a whole is most common in the early horizons. Type E is illustrated by Figure 3G.

The most striking feature to be noted in the distribution of all scraper forms is that they are more abundant in zones B and C than in Zone D. The absolute frequency in Zone C is greater than in Zone D, and the number is more than doubled from zones C to B. This increase with depth is perhaps more significant than the absolute frequency would indicate since the total frequency of all artifacts reaches a peak in Zone D. It would therefore appear that skin dressing was a more important activity in the earlier occupation than in the later.

A large group of crudely chipped implements is classified as choppers. It is difficult to be certain that all implements included in the category are deliberately fashioned choppers and not simply cores. Some, however, suggest that they are shaped according to a definite pattern and others show indications of usage. In their characteristic form a block of chert was selected and one edge sharpened by bold percussion flaking from one or both faces to produce a sinuous cutting edge. Most commonly, rectanguloid or tapering blocks of chert, whose original edges were smoothed through rolling, were selected and the edge sharpened. Infrequently, a chopper edge was produced on a rounded pebble of chert or the entire block of chert was flaked with one edge forming the chopper edge. The implements are extremely variable in size and shape, the latter apparently depending on the random shape of the pebbles found. In length the implements range from 46 to 127 mm., in width from 42 to 74 mm., and in thickness from 16 to 54 mm. It is assumed that these implements do not have a scraping or cutting function because of the jaggedness of the edge, but rather that they are striking or chopping tools. The implements are distributed through all the levels except the very deepest, Zone A, at DlEvIII. The variation in size and shape is illustrated in Figure 4.

The only remaining chipped-stone category into which specimens found at DlEvIII are grouped consists of the cores. These

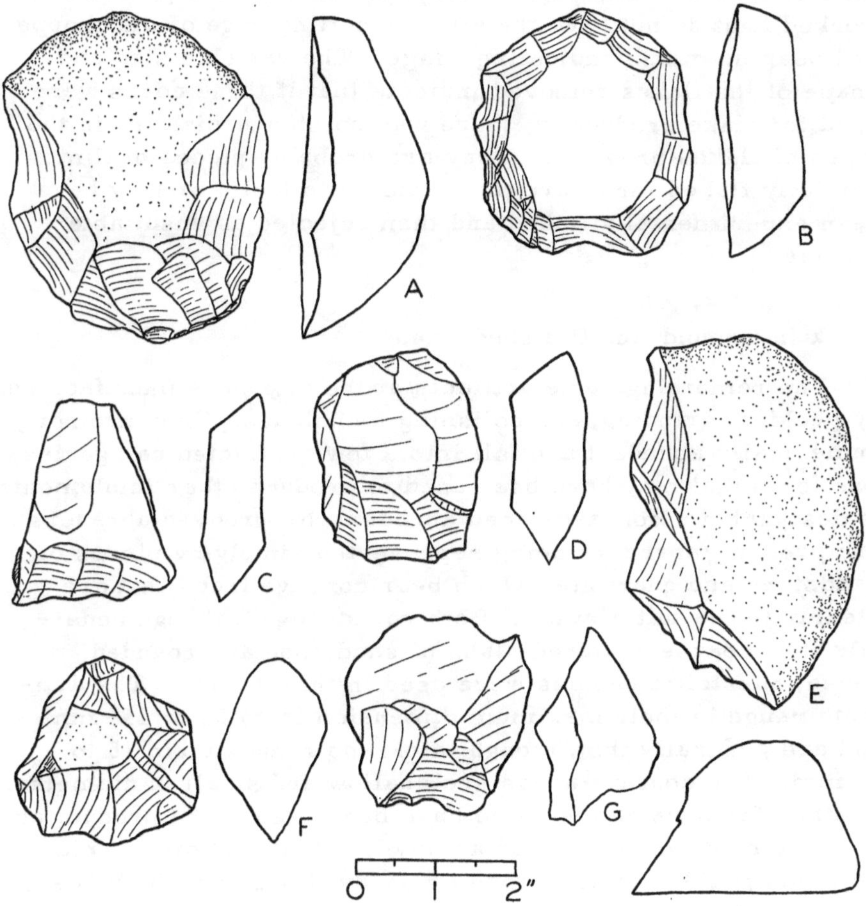

Fig. 4. Choppers, Site DlEvIII. Provenience:
Zone D (depth 32-64") — A-B;
Zone C (depth 64-104") — C, G;
Zone B (depth 104-136") — D, F;
Zone A (depth 136-180") — E.

are basically flat blocks of flint, either with a few flakes removed or with the entire surface shaped through bold percussion flaking. In no instance is there a shaping through pressure flaking that might suggest use as a specific tool. In only a few instances, primarily in the upper zone (D), are the cores carefully shaped into a generally ovate outline. These pieces of worked flint do not have the sinuous cutting edge of the choppers, and bear no marks indicating usage. The variable size and shape of the flakes removed indicate that if these cores were used for flake production, there was no standardization in the types of flakes produced. They are probably pieces of flint partially flaked for future production into tools, or they have been experimentally flaked and then rejected as unsuitable for use.

Work In Ground And Polished Stone

The remaining stone artifacts at the site were manufactured by pecking, grinding, and polishing techniques. They are not numerically abundant and fall into a few restricted categories. One form that may have been used to produce other implements is designated a concave-faced abrader. No grooved abraders are present, abraders being represented simply by pieces of sandstone and quartzite, which bear concave faces that are clearly the result of wear. Both round-edged, though generally flat, coarse-textured slabs of sandstone and rounded, dense, quartzitic pebbles were used in this fashion. The artifacts range in their maximum dimension from 53 to 154 mm. and are generally thin, though thickness ranges from 15 to 63 mm. The concave areas are shallow and small in diameter. Another form which may also have been used in the production of implements is designated an anvil. This consists of small, flattened pebbles of sandstone or sandy limestone which bear, on one or two faces, a small pecked area, rather shallow and circular in outline. Since the pecked holes are the only signs of usage it seems likely that the specimens represent anvils rather than pitted hammerstones. A single hammerstone consisting of a sandstone pebble, having a maximum diameter of 9 cm., was found in Zone D. The surfaces of this stone show abrasions due to hammering or pecking.

Grinding stones are much more common though no rigid distinction in form or type is to be noted in connection with the zone in which the forms occur. Throughout the entire deposit small grinding stones were found, usually consisting of small, rounded pebbles of sandstone showing wear or polish through use and ranging between 64 and 71 mm. in greatest dimension. This form of grinding stone is of an irregular outline and shows no indication of having been shaped. Manos, or larger grinding stones, ranging around 100 mm. in length, are largely confined to the upper levels. It is not possible to obtain full details because most specimens in this category are fragmentary. These fragments appear in general to have an irregular outline and either one or two grinding faces. There are no indications of small pecked areas in the center of the grinding face, a feature which commonly appears on manos from the other sites. Similarly, manos with a carefully finished outline, also a characteristic of the other sites, appear to be lacking. The only mano present in the early zones (A-C) is a specimen in Zone B. This implement, manufactured from fine-textured sandstone, has an irregular though generally ovate outline. The cross section is roughly plano-convex, the plane surface actually being slightly concave. The convex surface is rough, having been pecked into shape, and the implement shows no sign of use for grinding. This specimen, about 119 mm. in length, 86 mm. in width, and 61 mm. in thickness, may perhaps be an unfinished mano and thus indicate the presence of large grinding stones at the early period. Though absolute absence of manos during the early zones (A-C) is not certain, the relative frequency is certainly extremely low, a feature which continues through the later Zone D.

In none of the horizons is there any definite evidence of the presence of the large, oval-basin metate common in later horizons in this region. In Zone B, two small mortars are present. One specimen (No. R1403 in the University of Oklahoma collection) was manufactured in a boulder of cherty limestone about one foot in diameter and about half that in thickness. In this boulder a rounded cavity was pecked on two faces. Both cavities are about 9 cm. in diameter and 2 cm. deep. The other specimen (R1402) is a fragment of a sandstone mortar. The curvature of the grinding surface indicates a mortar having a diameter of about 12 cm., the grinding area being about 3.5 cm. deep. A third fragment from Zone D was manufactured from sandstone and could be part of either a metate or a mortar. The size of the fragment is insufficient to indicate the nature of the grinding surface.

The only polished stone artifact is a full-grooved axe from Zone B. The axe was manufactured from chert, probably the local Boone chert. Though the entire surface has been smoothed, the presence of small concave areas appears to indicate earlier shaping flake scars. The butt end is flattened and unworked and the cutting edge of the blade is missing, having been broken off. The groove encircles the specimen and is 22 mm. wide and 4 mm. deep. The dimensions of the artifact are as follows: length, 102 mm.; width, 62 mm.; thickness, 41 mm.

Small bits of hematite, both red and yellow-orange in color, were distributed throughout the deposit, appearing in all zones. These small fragments average 10 to 30 mm. in length and 2 to 3 mm. in thickness. They bear numerous, closely spaced scratches on the surface, suggesting that through a scraping process powdered material was obtained that could be used as a paint.

No implements of bone or shell were recovered in the section of the deposit considered in this report.

In the preceding descriptions no mention has been made of the type of material because of the general uniformity of the varieties of stone utilized. With one exception all the chipped-stone implements were made of chert, local varieties predominating. These include the mottled gray and white Boone chert which is to be found in the vicinity of the site and the white and pinkish chert of the large quarries in Ottawa County, the adjacent county to the north. Other varieties of chert are probably in large part accounted for through the utilization of river pebbles as sources of material. In Zone C, occurs a fragmentary implement manufactured from a black quartzite similar to that commonly found in Fourche Maline Focus sites in LeFlore County to the south.

B. THE CAUDILL SITE — D1Ca1. (Location: NE. 1/4 SW. 1/4 Sec. 13, T. 24 N., R. 23 E.)

The Caudill site is located in the drainage area of Honey Creek, nearly two miles above the junction of the stream with Grand River. An area of 5,900 square feet was excavated on the south bank of the higher, rolling land which here borders the flood plain, about one-half mile from the stream proper. Numerous springs in this region give Honey Creek a constant flow of water throughout the year, and the midden deposit excavated was situated at the point of junction of two spring branches. Honey Creek is one of the important local tributaries of Grand River, its drainage system extending well into the state of Missouri.

The soil consisted of a black humus at the surface, with gravel and rock inclusions that gradually increased in number with depth, the soil color changing slowly from black to a dark brown. At the point of maximum thickness of the deposit, located in square 4:2 of the grid of 10-foot squares, the refuse-bearing soil attained a thickness of 28 inches. Grid squares were numbered in the same manner as illustrated in Map 2 for site D1EvIII. In the absence of any natural soil lines that could be followed, the site was excavated in arbitrary, horizontal, 4-inch levels. Since the field had been under cultivation, the first level was begun at the base of the observable furrows, the levels being kept horizontal. The 28-inch thickness appeared to be sufficient for some changes to be revealed by the depth at which the artifacts were found. The description and analysis of material is therefore presented in terms of the level, numbered from top to bottom, in which the specimens were found.

The only cultural features in the midden consisted of an ash bed and a single cache pit. The bed of ash was irregular in outline and surrounded by brown soil, showing no indication of a prepared fire basin. The bed was 5 inches thick, and the horizontal dimensions were 3.16 by 1.25 feet. It was located .75 feet north and 1.25 feet east of the southwest corner of square 3:6. The cache pit, designated C1, was located 6 feet 5 inches north and 9 feet 4 inches east in square 2:6. It was circular in outline, straight sided, and had a flat base. The horizontal dimensions of the pit were 3 feet 7 inches by 3 feet 6 inches and the base of the pit reached 2 feet below the surface. Its contents consisted of unworked mussel shell, 40 fragments of bone (animal), and a single, broken, chipped-stone projectile point of Type A1. Since this cultural material was distributed through the fill of the pit, it probably consisted of refuse that gradually accumulated after the use of the storage pit was discontinued.

Pottery

Only 14 pottery sherds were obtained at the site. Six of the sherds are undoubtedly from a single vessel and the similarity of the others suggests that, in all, fragments of only two or three vessels are represented. The two vessels that could be identified definitely are of different pottery types.

Sections of a single rim were collected from levels 1 and 2 of grid square 2:2. They consist of a smooth ware, which had been tempered with fine shell, now completely decayed. Both exterior and interior are of a light tan and orange color. The core is black near the rim but in the lower portion of the shoulder it is light and uniform with the surface coloration. The rim itself has a gentle outward curvature. A small section of the lip indicates that it bore a decoration of hemiconical punctate impressions paralleling the ledge. The decoration on the shoulder of the vessel consists of 4 parallel, broad, incised lines bordered on the upper edge by dashes or hemiconical punctate impressions parallel to the incised lines. The exact shape of the impressions is not certain since the deep, bold incisions were smoothed over slightly while the clay was still plastic. This decoration is arranged in an angular band which probably continued around the shoulder of the vessel. The rim sherd clearly represents the Neosho Punctate type of the Neosho Focus though a smoothing over of the decoration is rarely encountered in this complex (Pl. IIIB). Two additional undecorated body sherds with a decayed shell temper, one of which was obtained in Level 2 of square 8:7 and the other in Level 3 of square 4:3, may be of the same pottery type.

The remaining sherds are of a Hopewellian or related Woodland type. Six of these are undecorated body sherds. All have a smooth surface, either tan or brown in color on both interior and exterior, with a black or gray core, or with a light exterior coloration and a dark interior. All have a grit temper consisting of crushed limestone and chert ranging from fine (around 1 mm. in size) to coarse (up to 4 mm.). The thickness of the sherds ranges from 8 to 13 mm. The decorated sherds are all from the same vessel and it is possible that the undecorated body sherds may also be from the same vessel as the decorated sherds. They indicate a vessel which has a nearly vertical rim and a slight expansion in diameter toward the shoulder. The lip is flattened and bears fine diagonal incisions on the outer edge. Particularly on the rim the surface shows traces of a smoothed-over cord roughening. A band of embossing placed 14 mm. below the lip encircles the rim. Below the nodes are vertical rows of the shallow impressions of a coarse, straight dentate stamp. The vessel wall thins from a thickness of 10 mm. at the lower section to 6 mm. at the lip. For an illustration of this type see Plate III A.

The sparsity of sherds in relation to the area covered by cultural remains, as well as their limitation to the upper part of the deposit, suggests that the site consisted largely of the remains of a preceramic complex. Of the two pottery types present, the Neosho Punctate type is clearly the later. Its relative age is demonstrated by its stratigraphic superposition on the Hopewellian type at other sites, and a recent age is postulated for it by the resemblance to Upper Mississippi types. The type may possibly represent the prehistoric culture of one of the historic tribes of the region, such as the Osage. Since the Hopewellian sherds represent an early ceramic type in the region, it is possible that they may have been trade pieces acquired while the site was still occupied by the nonceramic group. An analysis now in progress of material from the Cooper site, the largest Hopewellian site in the area, indicates that the pottery type found at DlCaI is not the earliest pottery type in the Woodland series, but represents a later variety. Since the Cooper site is located only two miles from DlCaI, it seems unreasonable to suppose that a nonceramic group could reside in such close proximity and not learn pottery making. If members of the group did acquire pottery by trade, we should expect it to be the earliest pottery made in the area. The only alternative explanation, therefore, since this did not take place, is that subsequent to the formation of the preceramic deposit, the site was visited by two distinct peoples. The sporadic camping of both Hopewellian and Neosho Focus groups appears to have resulted in the intrusion of a few sherds, and perhaps other artifacts, in the deposit.

Work In Chipped Stone

Projectile points are the most numerous of the chipped-stone artifacts which occurred in a variety of forms at this site. The typological categories conform to those utilized in the description of site DlEvIII, with the addition of several new types consisting of a series of small projectile points.

One specimen (Figure 7R) appears to give an indication of the manufacturing technique used to form some of the projectile points. Basically, this specimen has a pointed ovate form with a length of 67 mm., a width of 44 mm., and a thickness of 9 mm. One corner of the broad end bears a shallow notch. The specimen seems to represent an unfinished point, and if a corresponding notch were produced on the other corner, the resultant form would be a point of Type E2 with a convex blade and base. In this method of production the basic form appears to have been made first, while the notches or stem were the last part of the point to be formed.

TABLE III

Distribution of Projectile Point Types, Site D1CaI
Second column indicates distribution in terms of percentage within a given level

Type	Level 1 0-4 inches		Level 2 4-8 inches		Level 3 8-12 inches		Level 4 12-16 inches		Level 5 16-20 inches		Level 6 20-24 inches	
	Number	Per cent	Number	Per cent	Number	Per cent	Number	Per cent	Number	Per cent	Number	Per cent
A1	7	11.6	9	12.3	5	8.6	5	9.6	4	10.8	4	26.6
A2	7	11.6	10	13.6	7	12.0	7	13.4	6	16.2	4	26.6
A3	1	1.6	2	2.7	3	5.1	1	1.9	1	2.7	..	..
B1	6	9.9	9	12.3	11	18.9	13	24.9	3	8.1	..	..
B2	8	13.3	7	9.5	10	17.2	5	9.6	2	5.4	2	13.3
B3	..	..	1	1.3	1	1.7	2	3.8	1	2.7	1	6.6
C	4	6.6	4	5.4	5	8.6	4	7.6	2	5.4	..	..
E1	7	11.6	7	9.5	7	12.0	6	11.5	10	27.0	1	6.6
E2	4	6.6	6	8.2	3	5.1	3	5.7	6	16.2	2	13.3
G1	5	8.3	8	10.9	1	1.7	..	..	..	..	..	..
G2	7	11.6	5	6.8	4	6.8	2	3.8	1	2.7	..	..
G3	1	1.6	3	4.1	..	..	..	..	..	..	..	..
H	..	..	1	1.3	..	..	..	..	..	..	..	..
Unclassified	3	4.9	1	1.3	1	1.7	4	7.6	1	2.7	1	6.6
Total...	60		73		58		52		37		15	

For the projectile points of this site, the types present and their relative frequencies are given in Table III. With the exception of the Type G series, all of the types have been previously defined in connection with their presence at site D1EvIII. The difference in size between the small points, classified as Types G1, G2, and G3, and the large projectile points of the other types is suggestive of the difference which is assumed to be present between dart points and the points utilized on arrows. It is important to note in this connection that when the length of all of the points is plotted on a graph, a definite bimodal curve is formed. The small points are not the result of the gradual tailing off in size of the large points, but are a definite cluster of points around new concepts of size. This would suggest a functional difference among the types. It is also to be noted that the small points were concentrated in the upper half of the deposit, indicating that the projectile point complex had undergone a marked change approximately at the mid-point of the occupation of the site. Type G1 points are unnotched, lacking a distinct stem, and are not further subdivided since all are generally leaf shaped, pointed at one end, and have either a convex or straight base. Type G2 points have a small stem produced by diagonal notches. The body frequently is serrated. Type G2 points are differentiated by their proportions from Type G3: Type G2 points are proportionately narrow, whereas Type G3 points are proportionately broad and, in general, parallel those of types B1 and B2 in form, though they are of a diminutive size. In the matter of size, types B1 and B2 have a maximum length of 40 mm. or more, while Type G3 falls below 40 mm. in maximum length. Types G1 through G3 are generally rather crudely flaked, and though they are manufactured from small flakes the subsequent retouching is rough and irregular. Frequently a large portion of the original flake is left unmodified.

The variation in component features of the projectile points of site D1CaI is given in the trait list of Appendix I. Illustrations of the variation within the types is given in figures 5 and 6. The only points requiring specific comment are the variant forms not classified according to the established types. Three distinctive points are illustrated in Figure 6 T-V. Two long projectile points with proportionately long stems formed by shallow side notches were recovered from Level 1 (Figure 6 T, U). A somewhat similar form, equally long and narrow, has a stem formed by shallow side notches but of more nearly normal proportions for Type B1 (Figure 6 V). One unclassified form from Level 4 has a proportionately broad body with an expanding, rounded stem. Another point from the same level is similar to Type C, but has a straight-sided stem rather than a flaring one. The remaining unclassified forms lack a stem but are generally large and in proportions and size are more like the large projectile points than those of Type G1.

Details of the variation in mean dimensions of the projectile points are given in Table IV. The table is presented in terms of the typological categories in which the points are classified. In comparison with those of site D1EvIII, some types show a marked decrease in maximum length and width. In Type A1 and Type A2, the mean width and length of the points D1CaI are less, though the small series of points at D1EvIII makes interpretation of the significance of decreasing size difficult. Stem length

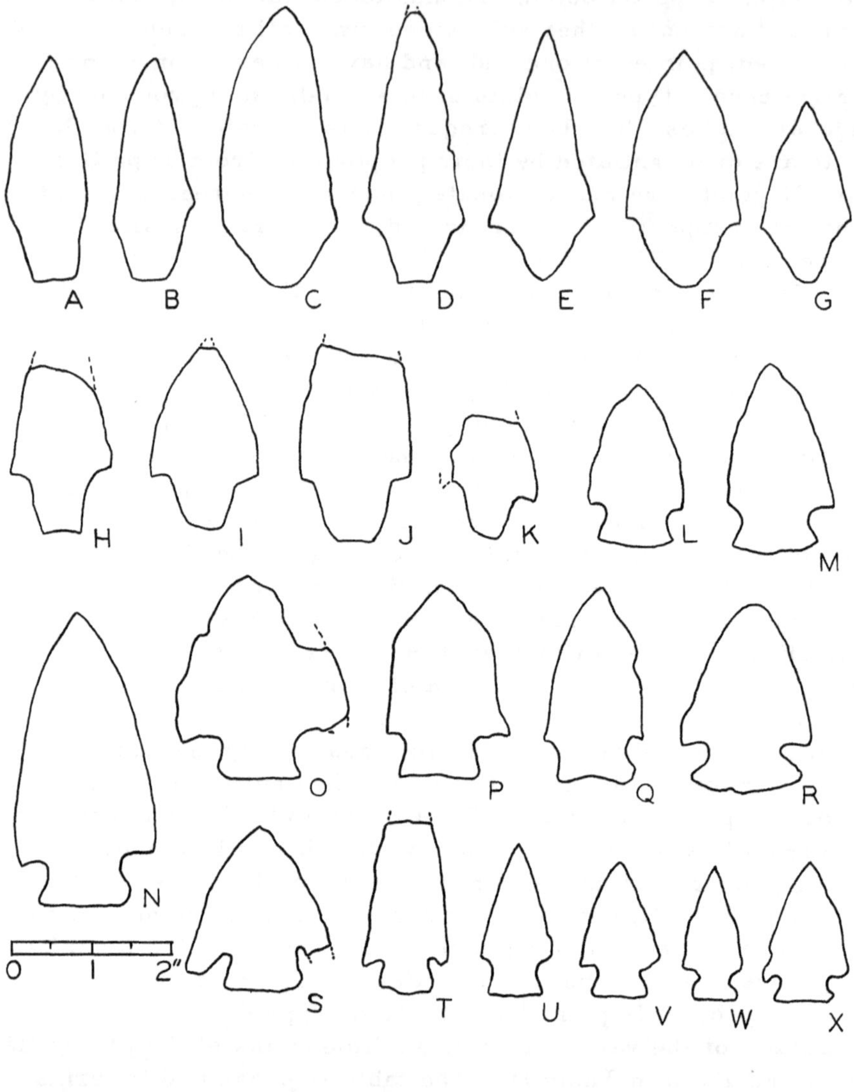

Fig. 5. Projectile Points, Site DlCaI. A-C — Type A3; D-H — Type Al; I-K — Type A2; L-Q, U-W — Type B1; R, T, X — Type B2; S — Type B3.

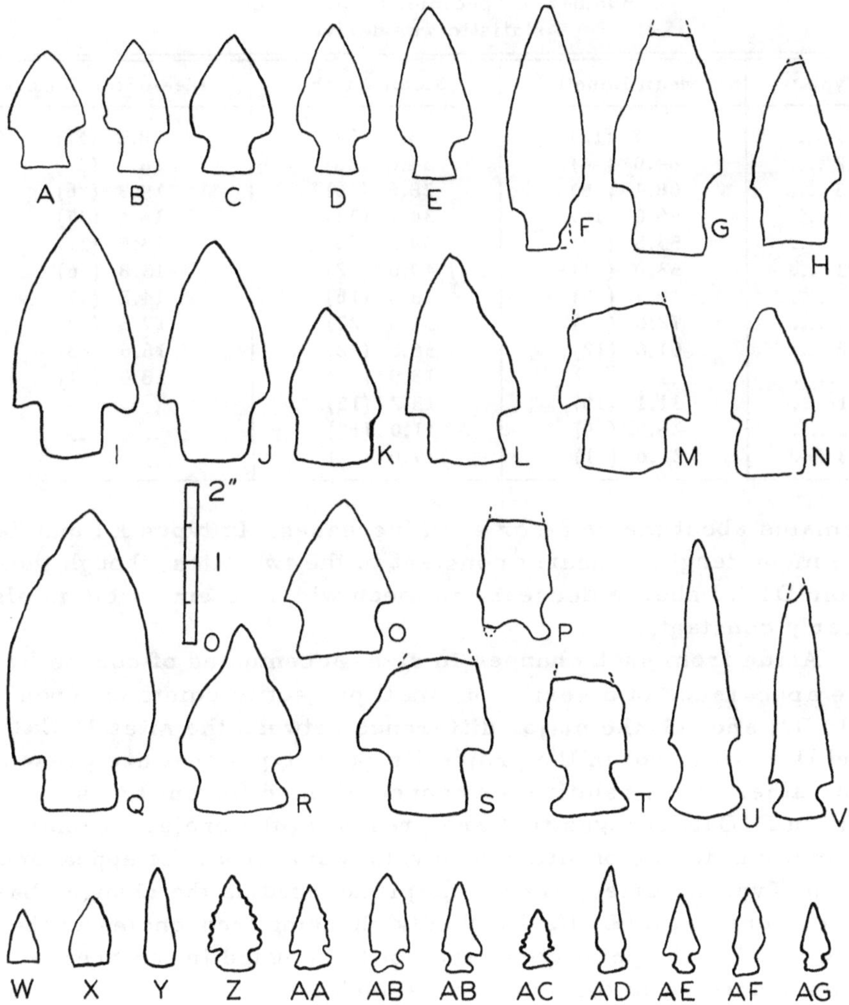

Fig. 6. Projectile Points, Site DlCaI. A-F — Type C; G-K — Type E1; L-O, Q-S — Type E2; P — Type H; W-Y — Type G1; Z — Type G3; AA-AG — Type G2; T-V — unclassified.

TABLE IV

Mean Dimensions of Projectile Points, Site DlCaI
Figures in parentheses following the mean indicate the number of specimens from which the statistic was derived

Type	Mean Length	Mean Width	Mean Stem Length
A1	68.7 (12)	33.1 (34)	20.2 (41)
A2	64.0 (4)	34.6 (28)	18.9 (32)
A3	68.4 (5)	28.6 (6)	19.7 (6)
B1	56.0 (16)	34.4 (33)	14.4 (37)
B2	53.5 (13)	39.0 (26)	13.5 (31)
B3	53.0 (1)	49.0 (2)	13.8 (6)
C	49.7 (7)	25.9 (16)	14.2 (17)
E1	72.5 (8)	34.5 (27)	17.6 (33)
E2	61.6 (12)	36.8 (22)	16.6 (23)
H	.. ..	13.0 (1)	18.0 (1)
G1	31.1 (10)	15.2 (15)	.. ..
G2	26.5 (9)	11.0 (19)	.. ..
G3	31.0 (1)	17.0 (1)	.. ..

remains about the same or even increases. In types E1 and E2 the mean length is nearly constant in the two sites, though those from D1CaI show a decrease in mean width. Stem length is also nearly constant.

Aside from such changes in size, accentuated of course by the appearance of a series of small projectile points of types G1, G2, and G3, the major difference between the sites D1CaI and D1EvIII is not in the projectile-point types that are present, but rather in the relative abundance of the different types. Within D1CaI, changes that are present in the projectile-point complex in terms of different levels, aside from the appearance of the Type G series, are not as pronounced as the changes between zones in D1EvIII. Markedly changing frequencies in the large projectile-point types are not to be noted in the breakdown according to the arbitrary 4-inch levels.

Only two bunts were present at D1CaI, both of which have a sharply rounded end. One example is illustrated in Figure 7D.

One general feature of the chipped-stone drills is that small forms appear to be characteristic of the top level (Level 1), but occur also in Level 2 in about equal numbers with the larger drills. The larger drills then continue through the deeper levels. Since most of the chipped-stone drills are broken, it is not possible to express this increase in size in

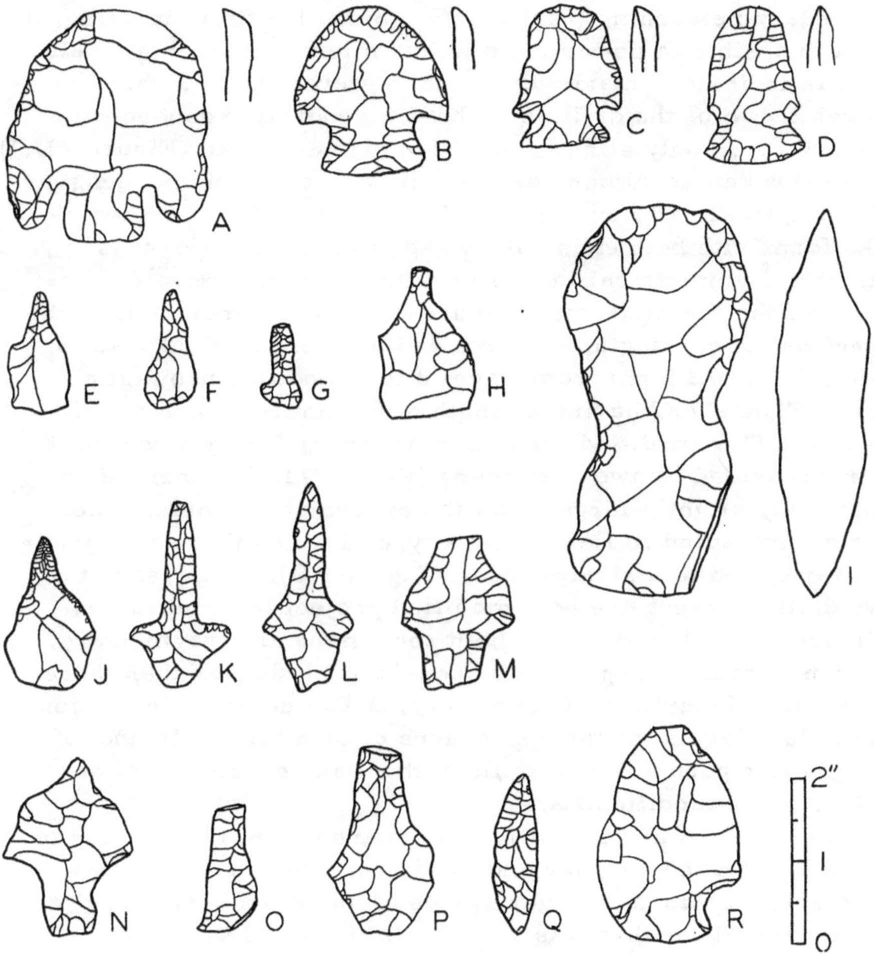

Fig. 7. Chipped Stone Implements, Site DlCaI. A-C — stemmed scrapers; D — bunt; E-H, J-Q — drills; I — chipped stone axe; R — unfinished (?) projectile point.

precise quantitative terms. Of the three drills present in Level 1, two have a generally rounded base which consists of an only slightly modified flake, one face bearing a sparse amount of secondary retouching (Figure 7 F, J). These specimens are unbroken and have a maximum length of 46 and 35 mm.; a maximum width of 29 and 16 mm.; and a maximum thickness of 5 and 3 mm. The third drill from Level 1, though of the same general form, has a base which is completely modified by secondary retouching (Figure 7 G). Since the tip is missing, it is not possible to obtain the maximum length, though a small size is indicated; maximum width, however, is 12 mm. From Level 2, two of the drills also have a generally rounded base formed by an only slightly modified primary flake (Figure 7 H, J). The unbroken specimen has the following dimensions: length, 37 mm.; width, 18 mm. In Level 2 there was found a needle-like form with both ends somewhat pointed. This form is slightly asymmetrical in outline with the maximum width occuring near the mid-point (Figure 7 Q). The dimensions of the specimen are: length, 49 mm.; width, 13 mm.; thickness, 5 mm. A second form from Level 2 is a modified projectile point (Figure 7 K) having a length of 56 mm., and a width of 31 mm. This modified form also occurs in Level 3, where it is represented by two specimens (Figure 7 L, N), their sizes being only slightly larger than the preceding example. They are accompanied in Level 3 by a type in which there is a gradual expansion to a straight base (Figure 7 O). In Level 5, the two drills present are both modified projectile-point forms (Figure 7 M, P), and though both specimens are fragmentary, their proportions appear to be considerably larger than those previously described. In summary, D1CaI contains indications in the late levels of the appearance of smaller drills and of the greater popularity of drills with a base consisting of an only slightly modified flake.

Knife forms are classified in a manner similar to those of D1EvIII, with the rougher and cruder specimens grouped as core knives. Since a larger series of unbroken knives is present at site D1CaI than was recovered at site D1EvIII these are divided according to size in the trait list and then classified according to basic shape. The range in form is illustrated in Figure 8 A-F and J-P. The series J-P indicates the manner in which presumable knife forms grade into a projectile-point size. The distinction between the two functional categories is difficult to make because of this gradation in size. One distinctive form needs special mention. This knife has a diamond-shaped outline and the edges bear a steep retouch forming an alternate bevel (Figure 8 I). The dimensions are as follows: length, 125 mm.; width, 35 mm.; thickness, 10 mm. It is represented by a single specimen at this site found in Level 1, although among Neosho Focus components it is an artifact type

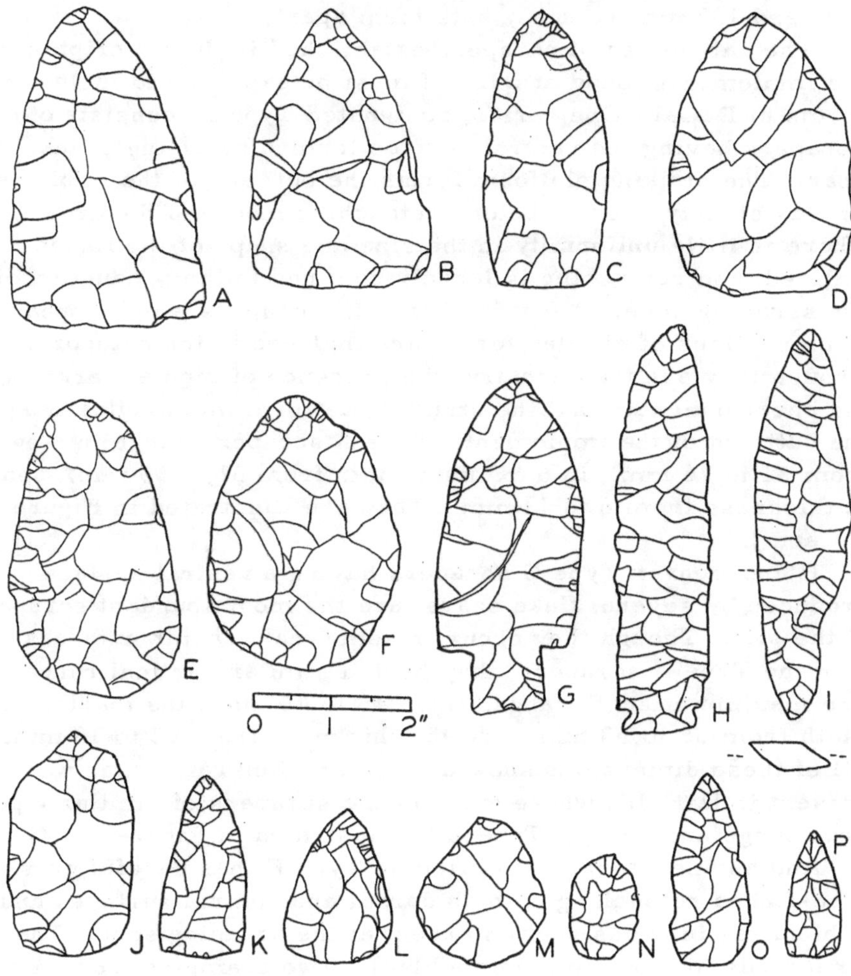

Fig. 8. Knives, Site DlCaI. A, C-F, J, L-N — knives; B — core knife; G-H — stemmed knives; I — diamond-shaped, alternate beveled knife of Neosho Focus type; K, O-P — knives or points.

of relatively frequent occurrence. Here it seems to be a chipped-stone implement of more recent provenience, one to be grouped with the few sherds of Neosho Punctate pottery type and considered intrusive at the site. Site D1CaI also contained two stemmed implements which are considered knives (Figure 8 G, H). Though paralleling the projectile points in form, the extreme length (107 and 132 mm.) readily sets them apart.

The categories of scrapers established in the description of the implements found at D1EvIII must be expanded to include all forms at D1CaI. One series, designated Type A, consists of scrapers having the ventral surface formed by a single flake scar. The striking platform forms the butt end of the implement or was clearly present before retouching modified the area. There is little uniformity in the size and shape of the flakes utilized, and retouching is largely confined to the production of the scraping edge. A few fragmentary scrapers which appear to be portions of similar forms are included in the category. Though they are fragmentary, the presence of ripple marks in the chert indicates that the striking platform was originally at the butt end of the implement. Type A scrapers range in length from 31 to 76 mm., in maximum width from 31 to 59 mm., and in thickness from 6 to 11 mm. They are illustrated in Figure 9A and J.

Plano-convex Type C scrapers having a ventral surface produced by several flake scars are the most abundant scrapers at the site. Though they occur in somewhat greater numbers than the Type A scrapers, they have a similar vertical range. The maximum length ranges from 46 to 73 mm., the maximum width from 38 to 53 mm., and the thickness from 12 to 16 mm. All of these dimensions show a much smaller range than was present in D1EvIII, where many of the scrapers of similar type were large and heavy. Type C is illustrated in Figure 9B-G.

Another new form, classified as Type F, has careful pressure-flaked retouching on both dorsal and ventral surfaces and is biconvex in cross section except at the scraping edge. The form tends to taper to a pointed butt. Two examples, however, have a straight fracture across the butt end as though the pointed section had been broken off. These fragmentary specimens tend to be considerably longer (73 mm. and 50 mm.) than the complete specimen which is only 43 mm. in length, 27 mm. in width, and 8 mm. in maximum thickness. Type F scrapers are shown in Figure 9K.

Two scrapers are not classified according to a fixed type. One consists of a section of a blade with one edge reworked into a scraping edge. The other scraper is a carefully finished implement with the dorsal surface completely retouched by pressure flaking. The ventral surface is formed by a single flake scar, the

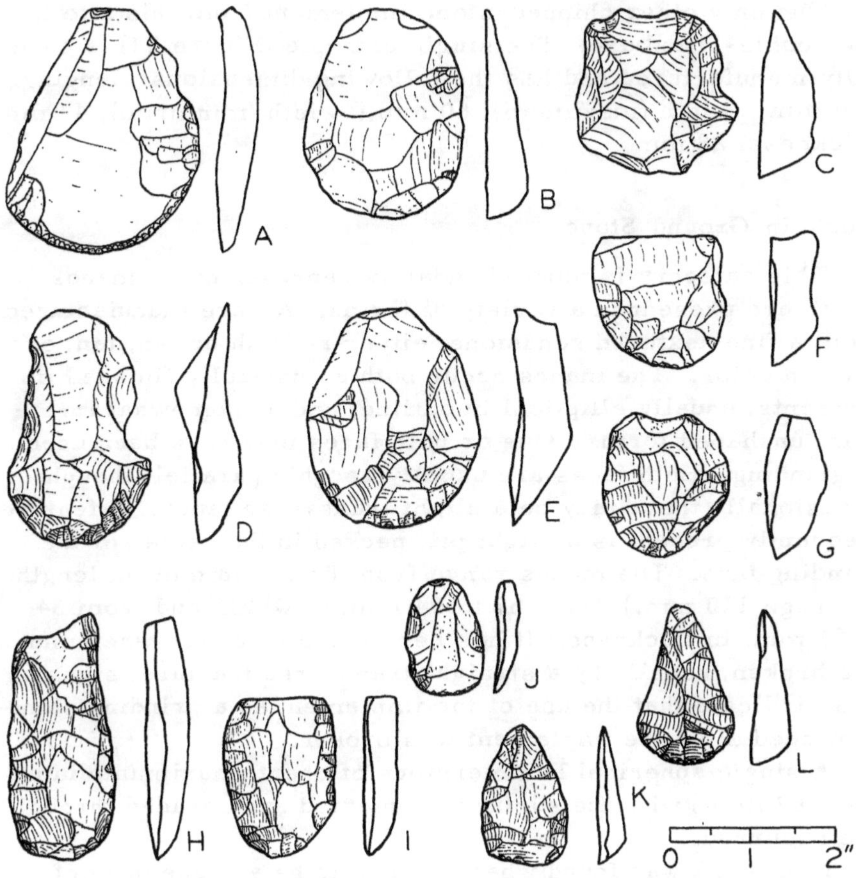

Fig. 9. Scrapers, Site DlCaI. A, J — Type A; B-G — Type C; H-I, K — Type F; L — Neosho Focus type scraper.

striking platform having originally been located at the butt end, though it has been removed in the process of shaping the scraper. The implement tapers from the scraping edge to a blunt butt end. The dimensions are: length, 47 mm.; width, 30 mm.; thickness, 10 mm. The implement is illustrated in Figure 9L. This form, like the alternate beveled knife, is commonly found in Neosho Focus sites and since it occurs as a single example and in Level 1, in all probability it represents a late intrusion.

Stemmed scrapers (Figure 7 A-C) are also common at the site.

The only other chipped-stone implement from this site is the double-bitted axe. The single example (Figure 7 I) is carefully manufactured and has the following dimensions: length, 120 mm.; width (maximum), 60 mm.; width (minimum), 42 mm.; thickness, 28 mm.

Work In Ground Stone

This category is most abundantly represented by manos which are present in a variety of forms. All are manufactured from a fine-textured sandstone, either reddish brown, tan, or gray in color. The manos occur both as carefully finished implements, usually elliptical in outline, and as somewhat irregular, unshaped forms. One or both faces may have been used in grinding. Both faces are usually roughly parallel, though occasionally there may be a slight transverse taper. A feature frequently present is a slight pit, pecked in the center of the grinding face. The manos range from 83 to 158 mm. in length (average 110 mm.), from 67 to 94 mm. in width, and from 34 to 63 mm. in thickness. It has been noted that even when manos are broken, usually by a straight transverse fracture, signs of wear indicate that the use of the implement as a grinding stone continued after the implement was broken.

A single spherical hammerstone of chert (maximum diameter, 67 mm.) with the surfaces contorted and abraded through use occurred.

In Level 2 was found what appears to be a crude bowl of sandstone, having a diameter of 98 mm. and a height of 38 mm. About one half of the bowl is present. The rim is rough and irregular, the interior partly smoothed, and the exterior rough and unshaped. It is difficult to be certain whether this is a manufactured form or a variety of natural concretion. The specimen is illustrated in Plate II G.

Work In Bone And Shell

A scraper consisting of a fresh-water mussel shell with the edges worn through use was found in Level 3 (Pl. III D).

Work in bone is represented by a single fragment of a bone awl. It consists of a splinter of long bone carefully smoothed along the entire length, though the butt end is missing. This artifact was found in Level 4 (Pl. III E).

C. THE G. G. McCONKEY SITE — D1McVII. (Location: NE. 1/4 SW. 1/4 Sec. 8; T. 25 N., R. 24 E.)

The G. G. McConkey site was located on the north side of Elk, or Cowskin, River close to a large spring which issued from the limestone hills bordering the river valley. The site was directly east of the county road which formerly skirted the foot of the hills. At this point the first terrace of the river was nearly an eighth of a mile in width and extended to within a short distance of the site, located on slightly higher ground. The higher terrace in the vicinity of the site was dissected by the stream which flowed from the spring through a deep meandering ravine some 15 to 20 feet below the level terrace surface. There was evidence of occupation on both sides of this stream and also on narrow spurs isolated by the stream's cutting action. Unit VII, the area for which an analysis is given, was the easternmost part of the site occupied and was not far distant from the farm house formerly located on the tract of land.

A midden area of 4,100 feet, which was excavated, yielded cultural material in local areas exceeding 2 feet in depth. However, the quantity of material below 20 inches was relatively slight. The midden area was excavated in 4-inch levels, the establishment of arbitrary levels again being necessary, since no natural stratification could be detected. No burials, cache pits, or hearths were observed in this area.

Animal bones were somewhat better preserved at this site than at the other preceramic components. In the series of fractured and split animal bones obtained, Dr. J. Willis Stovall, of the University of Oklahoma, has identified deer, turkey, opossum, and wild cat or lynx. Scattered clusters of fresh-water mussel shells present throughout the deposit indicate that these were also an item in the diet of the inhabitants of the site. The mussel shells, however, are not abundant and the series of animal bones is too small to give an adequate conception of the nature of the diet.

Pottery

As at site D1CaI only a small number of sherds, totaling 10, was found. All were concentrated in the upper part of the deposit;

there were none below 12 inches. All of the sherds might be classified as a Woodland variety. They have in common a coarse, angular grit temper consisting of particles of crushed limestone and chert ranging up to 5 mm. in size. The only variation in this feature is the presence in one sherd of grit temper consisting of limestone only, combined with what appears to be decayed shell and fine quartz sand, and the combination of fine quartz sand with grit temper in a second sherd. Thickness ranges between 4 and 9 mm., the average being between 6 and 7 mm. Surface colors, both interior and exterior, vary from a reddish to a mottled gray and black with the core generally black. Interior colors tend to be darker than the exterior colors. Surface treatment is varied, including smoothed, smoothed-over cord roughening, and a single fabric-impressed sherd. The latter sherd bears sharp, clear-cut, twisted-cord impressions and may represent paddle imprints though there is no overlapping of the impressions (Pl. IIIC). Only a single small rim sherd is present. It has a smooth surface and a rounded lip 5 mm. in thickness.

Despite the differences in surface treatment, the general appearance of the sherds suggests that they represent a single complex. Though they share some features, such as temper, with the Hopewellian pottery of this region, it is unlikely that they represent the same phase as the Hopewellian sherds of D1CaI. Varieties such as the "fabric-impressed" sherd are not present at the largest Hopewellian site in Delaware County, the Cooper site.

Vertical Distribution of Sherds

	4-inch Level		
	1	2	3
Smoothed surface	2	2	2
Smoothed-over cord roughened surface. . .	1	..	1
Fabric-impressed or paddled surface. . . .	..	1	..

Work In Chipped Stone

Projectile points are again the most abundant artifact and largely duplicate the forms present in the other sites discussed. The majority of the projectile points are large points of types A, B, C, and E (Figure 10). These were distributed throughout all levels at the site. A second important group of points consists of a series of small points grouped as types G1 to G3,

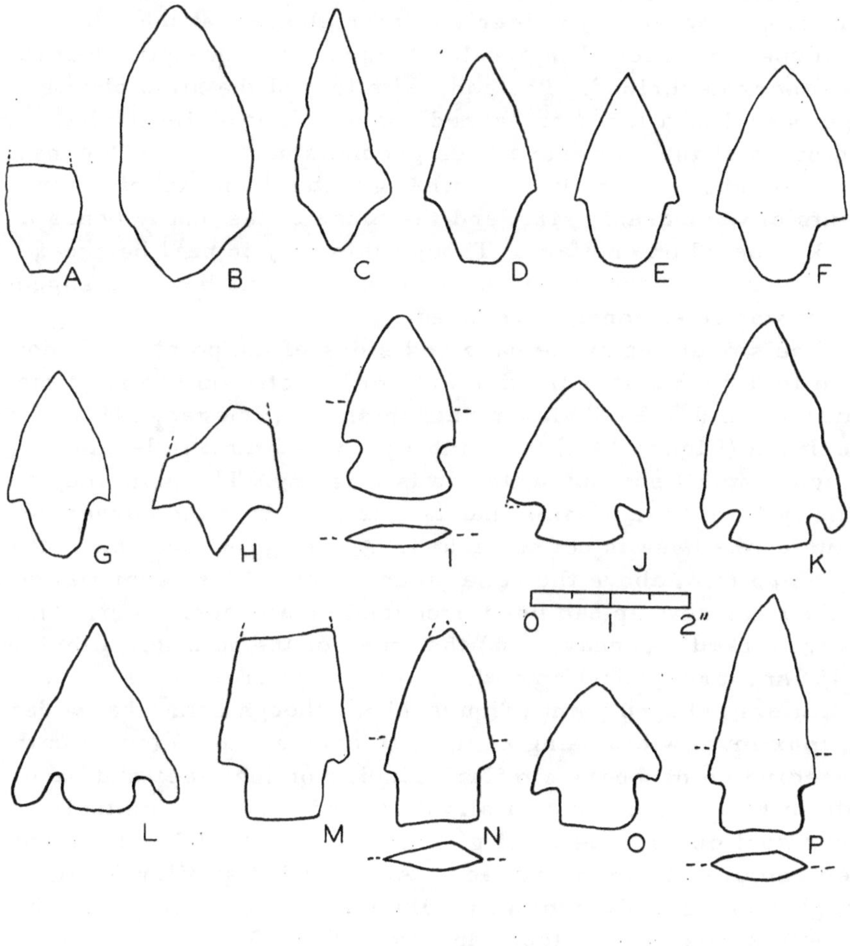

Fig. 10. Projectile Points, Site DlMcVII. A-B — Type A3; C-D — Type A1; E-H — Type A2; I — Type B1; J-K — Type B2; L — Type B3; M-O — Type E1; P — Type E2.

which showed a decided tendency to cluster in the upper levels of the site. The symmetry of the distribution of these points is broken particularly by a series of eight points of Type G3 found in Level 5, at a depth of 16 to 20 inches. It is to be noted that six of these points occurred at this level in a single square, 2:1. The clustering of points of this type in a restricted area suggests that, in part, the high frequency of the small points at this depth may have been due to secondary disturbance, such as the digging of a pit by later inhabitants of the site. The small points, as a whole, are clearly a later element at the site.

Type H was found in greater frequency at this site than at the others described. The general effect of the stem of this type is that of a lobed or "eared" base. Frequently the base and sides of the stem have been ground smooth. The thickness of the point is generally somewhat greater than that of other points of comparable size, and the blade occasionally bears a marked bevel on one face. Though this may in part be due to the thickness of the blade, the steepness of the beveling suggests that it was intentionally produced.

The smoothing of the base and sides of the point is not confined to Type H. It is particularly to be noted on two specimens which resemble Plainview points in shape (Krieger, 1947). One specimen (Figure 11 L) is a small point, 45 mm. in length, though a small portion of the tip is missing. The point may originally have been a somewhat larger one since the curvature begun at the base is not continued. A straight-sided contraction begins 23 mm. above the base, accompanied by steeper flaking, as though a new tip had been produced on a broken point. The base, markedly concave, and the sides of the point for a distance of 15 mm. are ground smooth. A fragment of the basal part of a similarly shaped point (Figure 11 K), though somewhat wider, the maximum width being 23 mm. in contrast to 19 mm. for the preceding point, bears similar grinding on the sides and base. Both of these points have a slight inward curvature on their lower section as a result of grinding. Channel flakes have not been removed from either face. A somewhat similar form, though lacking any grinding, is illustrated in Figure 11 J. The Plainview forms were found in levels 4 and 5.

Similar smoothing is also noted on Type C projectile points where 5 of a total of 19 points show the grinding. It is also occasionally encountered in other forms though not in marked abundance.

A small proportion of the points is not included in the described types. Two of these (from levels 2 and 4) have a flaring stem similar to the Type E2 form. The blade, however, has a gentle curvature merging through an indistinct shoulder area into the stem. The remaining 3 points have a straight parallel-sided stem similar to Type E1 forms. The stem, unlike the normal forms in Type E1, is proportionately short and

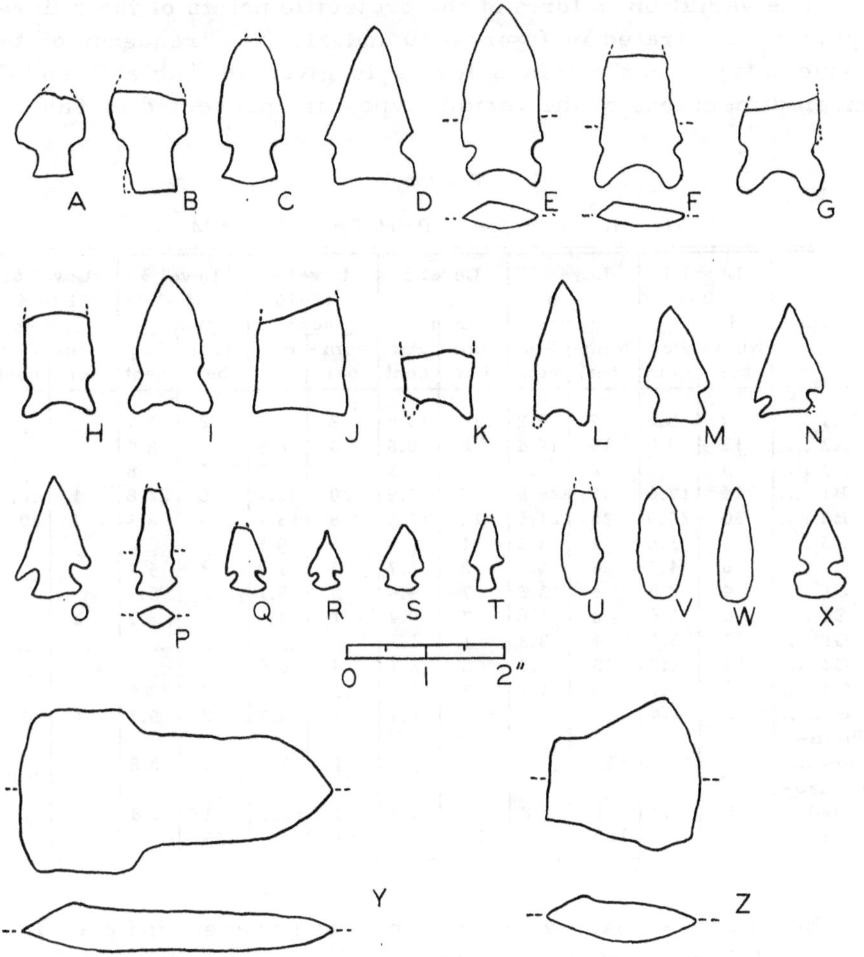

Fig. 11. Chipped Stone Implements, Site DlMcVII. A-X — projectile points: A-C — Type C; D-H — Type H; J — Plainview shape (?); K-L — Plainview type; M-O — Type G-3; P-T — Type G2; U-W — Type Gl; I, X — unclassified. Y-Z — axe blades (?).

narrow. The point, illustrated in Figure 11I, though tabulated as Type G3, bears a strong resemblance to the Type H variety. One of the small points tabulated as Type G2 (Figure 11X) is clearly a deviant form, resembling, with its horizontal side notches, late projectile points of the area. It possibly represents an intrusive point of a later complex.

The variation in form of the projectile points of the different types is illustrated in figures 10 and 11. The frequency of the various types in the 4-inch levels is given in Table V, and the mean dimensions of the various types are presented in Table VI.

TABLE V

Distribution of Projectile Point Types, Site DlMcVII

Type	Level 1 0-4 inches		Level 2 4-8 inches		Level 3 8-12 inches		Level 4 12-16 inches		Level 5 16-20 inches		Level 6 20-24 inches	
	Number	Per cent	Number	Per cent	Number	Per cent	Number	Per cent	Number	Per cent	Number	Per cent
A1	7	5.6	7	5.8	11	14.8	2	3.2	2	5.7	..	..
A2	13	9.5	15	12.4	8	10.8	4	6.5	3	8.5	..	..
A3	3	2.1	2	1.6	1	1.3	3	4.9	1	2.8	..	..
B1	24	17.6	31	25.8	17	22.9	20	32.7	8	22.8	1	20.
B2	30	22.0	26	21.6	13	17.5	8	13.1	3	8.5	1	20.
B3	5	3.6	4	3.3	1	1.3	6	9.8	..	..	..	..
C	6	4.4	6	4.9	2	2.7	3	4.9	2	5.7	..	..
E1	4	2.8	4	3.3	7	9.4	5	8.1	2	5.7	..	..
E2	5	3.6	2	1.6	7	9.4	1	1.6	2	5.7	2	40.
G1	7	5.1	4	3.3	1	1.3	..	..	..	..	..	..
G2	15	11.0	13	10.8	2	2.7	4	6.5	..	..	..	..
G3	16	11.7	5	4.1	3	4.0	..	..	8	22.8	..	..
H	2	1.4	..	..	1	1.3	3	4.9	2	5.7	1	20.
Plain-view	..	..	..	..	..	..	1	1.6	1	2.8	..	..
Unclassified	1	.7	1	.8	1	1.3	1	1.6	1	2.8	..	..
Total	138		120		75		61		35		5	

Bunts with a sharply rounded end were present in Level 3 (2), Level 4 (1), and Level 5 (1). Stems are produced by deep and shallow corner notches and the bases are round (3) or straight (1). The bunt is illustrated in Figure 13M.

Chipped-stone drills are present in considerable variety of form. In common with site DlCaI, small forms were found in the top levels (1 and 2) in association with larger forms which continued through the deeper levels. Another feature of the drills in the upper levels, also shared by site DlCaI, was the presence of drills whose base consists largely of an unmodified flake. A classification according to form yields the following categories:

1. This form has only a slight expansion to the base, often with a slight constriction immediately at the basal area so that

TABLE VI

Mean Dimensions of Projectile Points, Site DlMcVII
Figures in parentheses following the mean indicate the number of specimens from which the statistic was derived

Type	Mean Length	Mean Width	Mean Stem Length
A1	66.5 (13)	33.0 (43)	19.3 (47)
A2	63.8 (7)	35.0 (27)	19.9 (31)
A3	66.0 (1)	28.0 (8)	18.5 (8)
B1	51.5 (19)	33.0 (59)	14.6 (70)
B2	51.0 (12)	35.8 (35)	12.9 (41)
B3	60.5 (2)	38.2 (4)	12.0 (5)
C	49.5 (2)	24.2 (12)	14.7 (14)
E1	61.6 (5)	37.6 (14)	16.8 (20)
E2	70.6 (3)	37.4 (13)	16.3 (14)
H	54.5 (2)	27.2 (4)	8.5 (4)
G1	38.2 (5)	18.3 (11)	.. ..
G2	23.9 (12)	11.8 (23)	.. ..
G3	35.6 (10)	21.6 (21)	.. ..

the widest part is found above the base of the drill. The general appearance is that of a needle-like form, though it is pointed on only one end. In length this form ranges from 35 to 62 mm., in width from 12 to 23 mm., and in thickness from 6 to 9 mm. Drills of this form are completely retouched over the entire surface. They were present in levels 1 to 4 with a single specimen in each, except for Level 2 which contained two (Figure 12 T-U).

2. This variety has a gradual, but marked expansion to the base, the widest part of the drill being found at the extreme basal area, producing a general triangular form. The only complete specimen is 53 mm. in length; width ranges from 20 to 30 mm.; thickness from 7 to 8 mm. Nearly all of these specimens were carefully retouched over the entire surface though one specimen from Level 2 has a basal region largely formed by an unmodified flake with secondary retouching only at the edges. The form was found in levels 2 (1), 4 (2) and 5 (1) (Figure 12 V).

3. This form of drill has a sharp, angular expansion at the base forming a thin, T-shaped outline. The drills were carefully retouched over the entire surface. They range in length from 48 to 55 mm., in width from 23 to 31 mm., and in thickness

from 5 to 7 mm. A single example of this form occurred in each of levels 3 and 4 (Figure 12W-X).

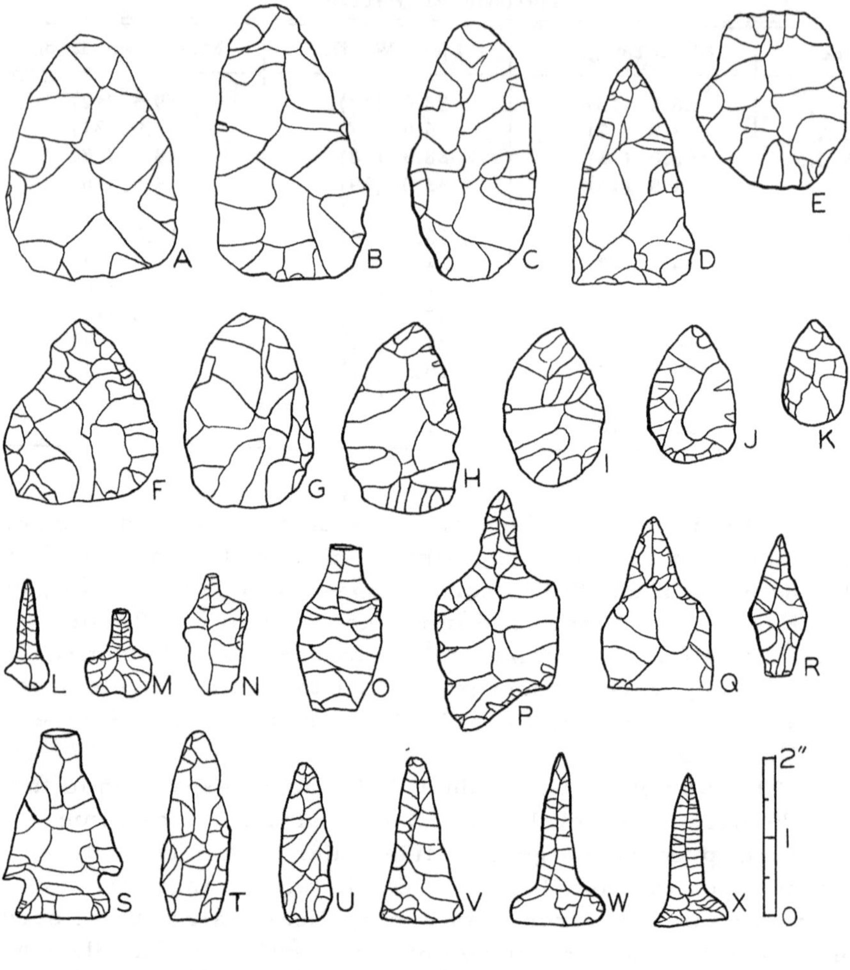

Fig. 12. Chipped Stone Implements, Site DlMcVII. A-K — knives. L-X — drills.

4. This variety has a roughly formed basal area, generally broader than it is long. Flaking varies from complete retouching over the entire surface to only slightly modified flakes. Specimens range from 36 to 58 mm. in length, from 13 to 36 mm.

in width, and from 4 to 11 mm. in thickness. One specimen (from Level 4) has a base formed by a straight fracture. The form was found as a single example in each of levels 2 and 4 (Figure 12G, M).

5. This form is similar to (4) except that the base is generally longer than it is wide. Flaking shows a similar variation, from complete retouching of the surface, to but slightly modified flakes which form the basal region. Specimens range from 58 to 77 mm. in length, 20 to 40 mm. in width, and 7 to 11 mm. in thickness. Two examples of the form were present in Level 2 (Figure 12N, P).

6. The final form consists of a drill having the appearance of a modified projectile point. Of the three specimens present, two — one from each of levels 2 and 3 — have a contracting stem while one from Level 2 has a stem formed by diagonal notches (Figure 12O, R, S).

The general features of the system of classification used in connection with the description of knives, core knives, and cores have already been presented in the discussion concerning the other sites. The forms parallel those of D1CaI except that stemmed knives and the alternate-beveled knife are lacking. Details of the distribution may be obtained from the appended trait list, and the forms are illustrated in Figure 12A-K. A transition, similar to that noted at D1CaI, of leaf-shaped knife forms to possible projectile points, is seen.

Considering the abundance of other chipped-stone forms, scrapers are not present in large numbers. They vary considerably, however, in size, shape, and method of manufacture.

Stemmed scrapers consist essentially of projectile-point forms which, instead of having a pointed blade, have a rounded-end blade retouched on the end from one face only to form a scraping edge. All of the specimens found have stems formed by shallow notches and the bases are convex, with one exeption which is concave. The implements range from 37 to 52 mm. in length, from 25 to 37 mm. in width, and from 7 to 9 mm. in thickness. The distribution at the site showed a clustering in upper levels. Five specimens were present in Level 2, and one specimen in Level 3 (Figure 13K-L).

Type A scrapers have a plano-convex cross section with the plane or ventral surface formed by a single flake scar. The butt end of many scrapers of this type consists of the striking platform remaining from the operation by which the flake was

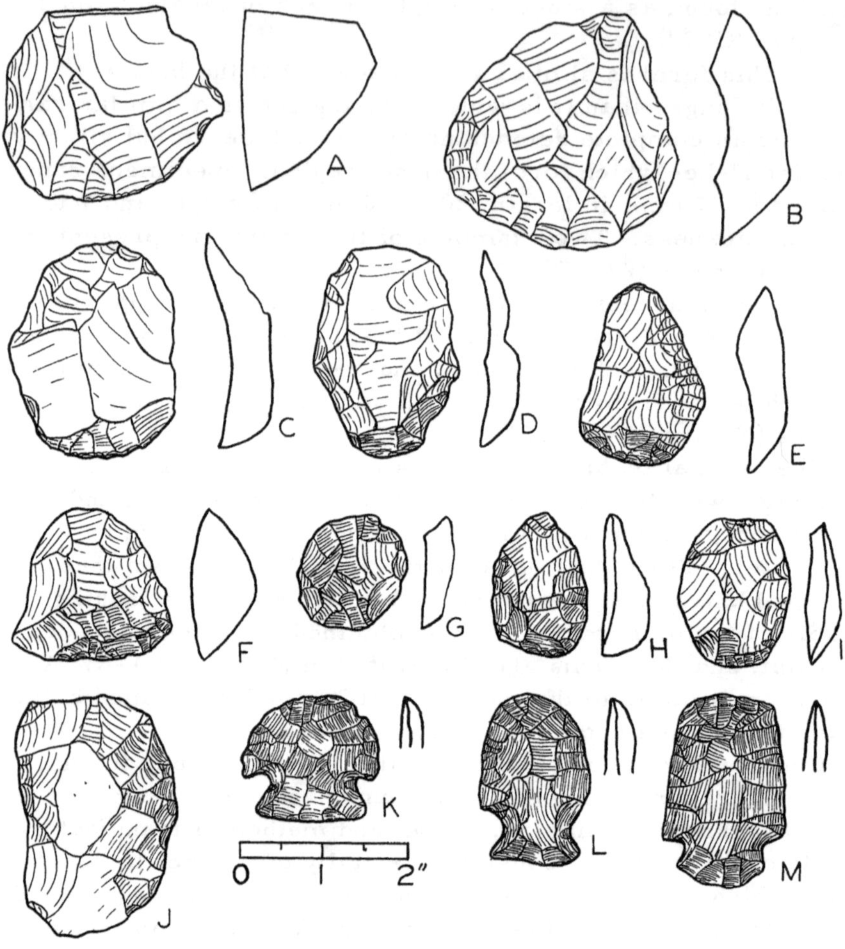

Fig. 13. Chipped Stone Implements, Site DlMcVII. A — scraper, Type B; B, D, F, H, J — scrapers, Type C; G — scraper, Type D; C — scraper, Type A; E, I — scraper, Type E. L, K — stemmed scraper. M — bunt.

produced. Two scrapers included in this type at DlMcVII have the striking platform removed by secondary flaking on the dorsal surface. One specimen (from Level 1) is a small scraper (38 x

33 x 6 mm.), which is completely retouched, with a scraping edge around the entire circumference of the roughly ovate implement. The second scraper of this type (Figure 13C), found in Level 4, is a larger implement (65 x 52 x 14 mm.), and has a steep scraping edge at one end of the ovate implement.

Type B scrapers, though also plano-convex and with a ventral surface formed by a single flake scar, lack a striking platform either still present or originally present at the butt end of the implement. The ventral surface of the single specimen present, which was found in Level 3, bears cortex, indicating that it was not formed at the time the scraper was fabricated. It probably was formed as a part of the original flat surface of the tabular blocks of chert which occur as seams in the limestone of this area. The ventral surface is roughly made, its appearance suggesting a modified core. The dimensions of the specimen are 66 x 58 x 38 mm. (Figure 13A).

Type C scrapers, the largest class at the site, are also plano-convex in cross section but the plane surface is formed by several large primary flakes. Shapes are extremely variable, though roughly ovate, and circular forms are most common. The size ranges are: length, 50-75 mm.; width, 29-69 mm.; thickness, 10-25 mm. (Figure 13B, D, F, H, J).

Type D scrapers represent a form in which an attempt was made to produce a carefully finished "disc" with a symmetrical outline and a carefully finished scraper edge encircling the implement. The two specimens in the category (from levels 2 and 5) are slightly ovate in outline with the plane surface bearing multiple flake scars. The size range is: length, 36-51 mm.; width, 32-39 mm.; thickness, 9-15 mm. (Figure 13G).

Type E scrapers, unlike the other forms, are biconvex in cross section. The scraping edge was produced by having a greater convexity on one face and by slightly "turning" the scraping edge. These scrapers vary in form, ranging from symmetrical elliptical and ovate to irregular forms. One specimen may be a fragmentary implement since the butt end was formed by a straight break. The size range is: length, 40-64 mm.; width, 33-50 mm.; thickness, 9-16 mm.

One scraper, not classified as to type, consists of an irregular plano-convex implement having one edge formed by a straight fracture and a scraping edge consisting of a concave, retouched area. The dimensions of the implement are 53 x 39 x 18 mm., the scraping edge being only 30 mm. in length. The implement was found in Level 3.

A fragment of a chipped, double-bitted axe was found in Level 1. The specimen has a maximum width of 76 mm., a minimum width in the constricted section of 51 mm., and a thickness of 30 mm.

Two unusual specimens suggest that they may possibly be blades that could be set in some form of a handle and used as a striking or cutting tool. One of these, illustrated in Figure 11 Z, was found in Level 6, and has a roughly triangular form though with the apex of the triangle truncated. In cross section the implement is biconvex and all edges are slightly battered. The dimensions of the implement are 50 x 49 x 11 mm. The second specimen (Figure 11 Y) was found in Level 2 and has a composite outline. The broader portion is roughly rectanguloid and extending outward from one long edge is a parallel-sided blade, which tapers abruptly to a pointed end. The edges of the rectanguloid section are worn or ground smooth, while the edge of the remainder of the implement is sharp. The cross section of the implement is biconvex, and its dimensions are 102 x 53 x 15 mm.

A few rough choppers were found at this site. Two of the specimens have a sinuous edge, the flakes at the chopping edge having been removed from both faces of the implement. One of these specimens is rather small and round in outline, apparently having been derived from a small pebble, since a portion of the cortex is present on both faces. The dimensions of this artifact, found in Level 3, are 60 x 59 mm. The other specimen with a sinuous edge, a large ovate form, bears primary shaping flaking on both faces. Its dimensions are 143 x 93 x 39 mm. The third chopper, found in Level 3, also has a roughly ovate, pebble form, a plano-convex cross section, and bears large primary flake scars that have been removed from one face only. These are the only flakes struck from the chopper and are present on the broad end of the implement. The dimensions of the specimen are 101 x 69 x 35 mm.

As at the other preceramic sites, the flakes found show little uniformity in size, shape, or manner of production. There are none that seem to represent intentionally prepared flake knives. Many of them, however, have small flakes removed from the edges, suggesting usage scars. A general ovate shape with length ranging from 44 to 61 mm. is common.

Work In Ground And Polished Stone

A single polished stone implement (Pl. IIIK), consists of an atlatl weight found in Level 3. The shape is that of a solid, rounded pebble form with one flattened face. The sides and opposing face are convex. From the flattened face which has dimensions of 33 x 37 mm., two parallel grooves, 2 mm. wide and deep, extend a distance of 25 mm. down each end. The material is a fine-textured granitic stone which bears a rather high polish. The over-all dimensions of the specimen are 49 x 43 x 33 mm.

Grinding stones and carefully finished manos are the most abundant of the ground-stone implements. They are roughly classified into two groups, one consisting of an irregular form in which little attempt was made to shape the implement, and the second consisting of a carefully finished mano with an elliptical outline. Both groups commonly have a small cavity pecked in the grinding surface. A variable feature is provided by the fact that either one or both faces have been utilized in grinding. The only deviant form has an elongated rectangular outline with sides that are nearly parallel and a rectangular cross section. Stones of this form have two grinding faces, one convex and one nearly plane. The elliptical form varies in actual outline from a nearly rectanguloid shape with rounded corners to an outline that is almost circular. In size the manos range in length from 65 to 135 mm., in width from 60 to 102 mm., and in thickness from 34 to 66 mm. The averages of these dimensions are as follows: length, 96.8; width, 76.7; thickness, 47.1. Manos were found throughout levels 1 to 6, though in much greater abundance in the upper three levels.

Abraders also are common. The variety most frequently encountered consists of irregular blocks of sandstone ranging from small to large with faces bearing shallow concave areas resulting from the use of the stones as abraders. Broken manos were often utilized in such a manner. A single abrader bears one groove across its face. The groove is small and narrow (3 mm. wide, 2 mm. deep), and probably was used for bone implements rather than as an arrow-shaft straightener. The single grooved abrader was found in Level 1. Spherical hammerstones consisting of contorted nodules of chert are also present. Another artifact type is classified as an anvil. These artifacts have one or more shallow, round or oval cavities pecked in their surfaces. This appears to be the only section of the implement used in any manner, so that they are not to be considered pitted hammerstones. Small, oval-basin metates were utilized with the manos and grinding stones.

Artifacts Of Worked Bone

This category is represented simply by flaking tools made of deer ulnae and bone awls. The flaking tools have the projecting shaft of the ulna ground smooth to a rounded tip, the only workmanship on the bone being the rounding of the end. The bone awls were manufactured from splinters of animal long bone. Since the butt ends of the specimens are missing, measurements of length cannot be given. With one exception, the entire length of the shaft present is completely smoothed and polished. The exception, a single specimen found in Level 4, has only the tip smoothed and worked (Pl. III G). Completely smoothed splinters were found in levels 2 and 3. The deer ulna flaking tools were present in levels 2 and 5 (Pl. III I).

II. COMPARATIVE ANALYSIS OF THE OZARK MATERIAL

A. SEQUENCE IN THE OKLAHOMA PRECERAMIC COMPONENTS

The excavation technique utilized in the Oklahoma sites was the removal of the deposit in arbitrary 4-inch levels following the nearly horizontal surface contours. This procedure was followed because of the absence of indications of natural stratigraphy. Such a technique assumes an accumulation of the deposit in nearly horizontal layers. Since any cultural sequence postulated for the sites must rest largely upon the interpretation of the mode of formation of the middens, it is essential that this hypothesis be tested. While natural stratigraphic breaks or non-occupational strata are lacking, the abundance and distribution of artifact types may contribute data on the manner in which the midden accumulated. We shall, therefore, first examine the sites from this viewpoint.

At site D1EvIII eleven feet of deposit accumulated during the preceramic period. This thickness of the deposit facilitates the determination of the sequential development of the archaeological complex. In tabulating the frequency of specimens found in the arbitrary 4-inch levels in which the site was excavated (Table I), it was noted that two period of intensive occupation were indicated by a greater frequency of artifacts and that each of these periods was preceded by a section of the deposit containing relatively few artifacts. This varying frequency of artifacts could be traced square by square across the deposit in the deep row selected for analysis. Since the levels in which high and low frequencies of artifacts were found tend to coincide with little variation in vertical position in each square, this was thought to indicate an essentially horizontal accumulation of this section of the deposit. Furthermore, with this established, the typological sequence indicated at this site gives a standard against which the other sites can be compared.

At both D1CaI and D1McVII the deposits were relatively thin, not exceeding two feet in thickness. Within this 2-foot section we found no marked alternation of intensity of occupation corresponding to that of D1EvIII. Both sites had a larger number of artifacts in the upper part of the deposit with a gradually decreasing frequency toward the lower levels. Since the surface contours of both deposits were nearly horizontal, it seems unlikely that the mode of deposition in only two feet of midden could be other than a horizontal accumulation. The major problem is, rather, to determine to what extent cultural activities, such as the digging of cache pits, or rodent activities, might have disturbed the horizontal strata. It is in this respect that the distribution of artifact types may contribute some information.

The few sherds found at the two sites, on both internal and comparative evidence, may be attributed to later complexes. The number of sherds found at the sites in relation to the number of stone implements gives a ratio far below the ratio of sherds to stone artifacts in definitely ceramic sites in the region. This situation may indicate the first appearance of ceramics at a site when, as a new cultural element, its frequency was low. If such a situation existed here, it is to be expected that all of the sherds would be of a generally similar type. There is, however, little uniformity in the type of sherds present. One in particular, the Neosho Punctate type, found at D1CaI can be shown by stratigraphic evidence at other sites to be one of the latest pottery types in the area. Other sherds at D1CaI may be classified as Hopewellian in type, and distinct from the pottery at D1McVII, which is a variant Woodland type. The presence of at least three distinct pottery types seems to indicate that the sherds represent sporadic accretions to the middens at varying time periods, and not a single late period transitional to a ceramic phase. In all probability a few stone implements were deposited on the sites at the same time as the sherds, though only a few of these can be detected with certainty. These include two specific forms normally found in the Neosho Focus associated with the Neosho Punctate pottery: a diamond-shaped knife with an alternate bevel and an end scraper which is carefully flaked to a pointed butt end. Both stone-implement types appear at a late time period in the Plains area as a whole. These stone implements and the sherds are considered the latest increments at the two sites and should therefore appear in the topmost levels. Their actual vertical distribution is shown below.

	Frequency, Site D1CaI						Frequency, Site D1McVII					
Level:	1	2	3	4	5	6	1	2	3	4	5	6
Sherds (all types)	2	7	4	1	..	..	3	3	3	..	..	..
Alternate beveled knife	1	..	..	..	..		..	..	..	..	..	..
Neosho Focus scraper	1	..	..	..	..		..	..	..	..	..	..

This vertical distribution, with a marked scatter over at least a foot, suggests a mixing of the deposits. In view of this, a detailed analysis of the total complex in terms of the 4-inch levels seems questionable. To consider further the nature of the situation, we may examine the vertical distribution of the projectile points in the 4-inch levels at D1CaI and D1McVII. The projectile points are not only the most abundant artifact but should also be sensitive indicators of change. That changes in popularity of types occur with changes in depth, and consequently with changes in time, has already been demonstrated in connection with the description of the material found at D1EvIII, where the frequency of types in the superimposed zones was tabulated (see p. 14). The frequency and percentage of projectile-point types in a given 4-inch level at the two remaining sites are tabulated in Table III for D1CaI on page 34, and in Table V for D1McVII on page 50.

The marked trends in varying popularity of projectile-point types present in D1EvIII occur in relation to points of Types A2 and E1. In the four zones, Type A3 increases from 0 per cent in the lowest section, Zone A, to 8 per cent in zones B and C, and culminates as 51 per cent in Zone D. There is a corresponding decrease in popularity of Type E1 from bottom to top of the deposit, the range being from 100 per cent in Zone A through 62, 50, and 13 per cent in zones B through D, respectively. These trends are not duplicated at D1CaI and D1McVII. There is a suggestion, however, of the continued decline in popularity of Type E at both sites. The most striking example of a projectile-point type which varies in frequency with depth is found in a series which is present at D1CaI and D1McVII but which is lacking in D1EvIII. This consists of a group of small projectile points averaging around 28 mm. in length and classified as Types G1, G2, and G3. Since the distribution of these points clustered in the upper levels (predominantly in the upper foot, though continuing in smaller quantities in lower levels), they are obviously a late component as, indeed, are small points in the Plains area. While their distribution coincides in part with the distribution of sherds, as far as depth is concerned, they are not necessarily to be considered in association with the ceramic material. Though similar projectile points were found at the two sites, the sherds from the same two sites represent distinct complexes. Furthermore, the abundance of the points is out of proportion to the number of sherds. At D1McVII, for example, while only 10 sherds were found, there were 76 projectile points of the Type G series.

The vertical distribution of the Type G series at the two sites is essentially the same, suggesting an introduction of the small projectile point around the mid-point of the occupation of the sites, followed by a gradual increase in popularity in the latest preceramic period. The curve in increasing popularity parallels that demonstrated in other regions for utilitarian artifacts, such as pottery types following their introduction or development. The parallelism in increasing frequency of Type G points in the upper levels at both sites suggests that the disturbance indicated by the distribution of the sherds did not materially affect the general trend in projectile-point types. Disturbance, however, has affected even the lower levels to a certain extent. In D1McVII it may be noted that there were eight points of Type G3 in Level 5 and none in Level 4. Examination showed that six of these points occurred at this level in a single square, 2:1. The cluster of points of this type in a restricted area suggests that in part the high frequency of the small points at this depth was due to secondary disturbance.

According to the analysis presented above, the deposits have been subjected to minor disturbance by cultural or animal activities, though general developmental trends can still be detected. Many specific types do not show a uniform growth or decline in popularity, a fact which may be attributed either to the disturbance or to an intermittent occupation of the site over a long period of time. Such an occupation would probably not leave a complete picture of the development of the complex. In view of this condition, it seems necessary to consolidate the contents of several 4-inch levels and operate in terms of a general phase or period. The presence of small projectile points of the Type G series, then, serves to differentiate the top one foot of the deposit at sites D1CaI and D1McVII from the lower portion of the deposits. The presence of several types of small points is probably of greater importance than the simple presence of a new form since their small size may indicate the introduction of a bow and arrow in contrast to the use of the spear thrower (see pp. 14, 34). This may be used as the diagnostic feature in projectile points to distinguish the latest preceramic phase, designated Period C. The lowest one foot of the deposits at D1CaI and D1McVII, is quite similar to the top zone (Zone D) of the preceramic phase at D1EvIII. The deposits are sufficiently similar to permit grouping as another period, Period B, which obviously, through the stratigraphic evidence, precedes Period C in time. As the remaining and earliest period, Period A, we have the lowest deposits at D1EvIII, zones A-C, which are stratigraphically below Zone D. On typological grounds Zone D is included in Period B. In order to see how the cultural content of these three periods differs as a whole, a trait list for the periods (Table VII) is given.

It is difficult to evaluate many of the changes indicated in Table VII. In most artifact categories, the number of specimens is so small that some of the typological distinctions between periods may be a result of an inadequate sample. Nevertheless,

TABLE VII

Trait List of Preceramic Periods in Northeastern Oklahoma

	Frequency					
	Period A	Period B			Period C	
	DlEvIII Zones A-C	DlEvIII Zone D	DlCaI 12-24 in.	DlMcVII 12-24 in.	DlCaI 0-12 in.	DlMcVII 0-12 in.
Projectile point types						
A1	1	2	17	7	24	36
A2	3	2	13	4	21	25
A3	1	..	2	4	6	6
B1	5	6	16	29	26	72
B2	4	34	9	14	25	69
B3	..	3	4	6	2	10
C	1	..	6	5	13	14
E1	32	9	17	7	21	15
E2	3	11	11	5	13	14
G1	..	..	..	..	14	12
G2	..	..	3	4	16	30
G3	..	..	..	8	4	24
H	3	2	..	2	1	..
Plainview form	..	..	..	2	..	..
Unclassified	1	3	6	2	5	3
Bunt						
Sharp, rounded end	1	1	..	2	1	2
Blunted, rounded edge	1	..	..	..	..	..
Drill						
Gradual, irregular expansion to base	..	1	..	4	2	5
Distinct, roughly rounded base	1	..	..	..	5	2
T-shaped form	1	..	..	1	..	1
Modified projectile point	..	..	..	2	2	3
Elongated base form	..	..	1	..	3	..
Knives						
Large knives (80 mm.)	..	3	6	1	8	1
a) Ovate	..	..	3	1	5	1
b) Ovate-acuminate	..	3	1	..	1	..
c) Distinct base	..	..	2	..	2	..
Medium sized (50-80 mm.)	..	..	4	1	7	10
a) Ovate	..	..	1	..	1	2
b) Ovate-acuminate	..	..	3	..	1	7
c) Distinct base	..	..	..	1	2	1
d) Asymmetrical	..	..	..	..	3	..

TABLE VII (Cont.)

	Frequency					
	Period A	Period B			Period C	
	DlEvIII Zones A-C	DlEvII Zone D	DlCaI 12-24 in.	DlMcVII 12-24 in.	DlCaI 0-12 in.	DlMcVII 0-12 in.
Knives (cont.)						
Small knives (50 mm.)	..	..	1	1	2	3
a) Ovate	..	..	1	..	1	..
b) Ovate-acuminate	..	..	..	1	1	3
Knife fragments (base)						
a) Rounded base	14	24	16	12	12	27
b) Distinct base	7	6	3	7	7	10
Core knives	20	19	4	10	7	18
Cores	39	72	7	14	16	61
Stemmed scraper	2	..	5	..	4	6
Side scraper	2	1	..	1	..	2
Type A scraper	..	..	2	1	3	1
Type B scraper	4	1	..	..	..	1
Type C scraper	5	2	1	2	7	7
Type D scraper	..	..	..	1	..	1
Type E scraper	6	1	..	1	..	7
Type F scraper	..	..	..	..	2	..
Concave-edge scraper	..	..	..	..	..	1
Scraper, unclassified	..	..	..	..	2	..
Chipped axe, double-bitted	..	..	..	..	1	1
Choppers	11	15	..	1	..	2
Hoe (?)	..	..	..	..	..	1
Concave-faced abrader	7	3	..	2	..	7
Hammerstone	..	1	..	1	..	1
Small grinding stones	7	4	..	..	..	..
Large grinding stones (manos)	1(?)	5	12	12	31	67
Stone bowl (crude)	..	..	..	..	1	..
Full-grooved axe	1	..	..	..	..	..
Polished stone atlatl weight	..	..	..	..	..	1
Grooved abrader	..	..	..	..	..	1
Anvil	1	..	..	1	..	4
Shell scraper	..	..	1	..	..	..
Bone awl, splinter type	..	..	1	1	..	3
Deer ulna flaking tool	..	..	..	1	..	1

it is unlikely that at any single preceramic site the quantity of stone implements would be in excess of those recorded for the three sites described in the preceding section. Validation of the temporal changes, tentatively suggested, will probably come by obtaining a similar distribution of artifacts in other small components. In the meantime, we are justified in indicating what appears to be the manner in which the preceramic complex evolved in the three sites under discussion. The material from these sites has been grouped into three sequent periods, rather than into distinct complexes. In evaluating the material, a definite impression of cultural continuity is given by the persistence of artifact forms. The characteristics of the three periods are briefly summarized below.

Period A is represented only by the deep levels at site DlEvIII. Large, stemmed points are the most abundant of the projectile points and include side-and corner-notched forms (types B1, and B2), contracting stem points (types A1, A2, and A3), a flaring stem type (Type C), points with a broad, parallel-sided and slightly expanding stem (types E1 and E2), and a form having an expanding stem and lobed base (Type H). The distinguishing features of the points of this period are the presence of a small series with a proportionately broad blade, points with coarse serrations on the blade, and a relatively high proportion of points with a distinct, beveled blade.

Bunts are present with both a sharp, rounded edge and a blunted edge. The chipped-stone drills, which are relatively large, include both a distinct, T-shaped form and one with a roughly rounded base. Knives, though abundant, are fragmentary so that extensive information on size and shape cannot be given. Crude knives (core knives) and cores are also abundant. Scraper forms represented are stemmed scrapers, side scrapers, scrapers whose ventral surface is formed by a single flake scar though this scar does not constitute a primary flake deliberately detached from a core in the requisite shape (Type B), scrapers whose ventral surface is formed by a plane surface composed of several primary flake scars (Type C), and scrapers roughly biconvex in cross section with an end "turned" to form a scraping edge (Type E). Implements with a boldly flaked edge, designated choppers, are also common.

Ground-stone implements are represented by small, concave-faced abrading stones, stones bearing a small concave area pecked in the surface (anvils), and small grinding stones consisting of unshaped, flattened pebbles ranging between 64 and 71 mm. in length. The small grinding stones may have been used in small mortars, pecked in large blocks of sandstone, which are also present. A single large stone, resembling shaped manos of a later date, is tentatively classed as a grinding stone. Although this specimen is roughly pecked into shape it bears no marks of use. The single polished-stone implement present consists of a full-grooved axe, roughly shaped in chert.

Period B is thought to be represented by the topmost preceramic section at D1EvIII and by the lowest one foot of the deposits at D1CaI and D1McVII. Essentially the same projectile points are present in this period, though in different proportions. Additional types found include a form with a deep notch originating in the basal section of the point (Type B3) and two types of small points both with a small stem formed by notching (types G2 and G3). The latter types are present only at the close of the period and may represent intrusions from the next period. Two projectile points similar to a Plainview type (Krieger, 1947) were found at D1McVII.

The only form of bunt present has a sharp, rounded edge. Chipped-stone drills appear in a greater variety of forms, which include a type having a gradual, irregular expansion to the base, drills produced from a modified projectile-point form, and a variety having an elongated basal area. New types added to the scrapers include a form having a ventral surface consisting of a prepared single flake scar (Type A), and disc-shaped scrapers (Type D). Choppers are present in large numbers only in Zone D of site D1EvIII, which in many respects appears closer to the Period A complex.

In the ground-stone complex large grinding stones, including carefully shaped manos, are relatively common and outnumber the small grinding stones present only in Zone D of D1EvIII. Hammerstones also belong to this period. No artifacts of polished stone were found.

Only a single implement of shell, a mussel shell used as a scraper, is present. Bone tools include awls manufactured from splinters of long bone and a flaking tool formed from a deer ulna.

Period C represented by the top one foot of the deposit at both D1CaI and D1McVII parallels closely the artifact inventory of Period B. The same projectile-point types are represented, though again, in different proportions. The single addition is another small projectile-point form consisting of a small, unnotched point (Type G1). The Type G points have a markedly higher frequency.

Though chipped-stone drills similar to those of earlier periods are present, there is also a series of small implements, frequently with a base consisting of a slightly modified primary flake. One new type of scraper is added to the series, a form which tapers to a point at the butt end, and bears pressure retouching on both faces (Type F). A single scraper having a concave edge is also placed in this period. Two chipped-stone forms appearing for the first time in this period are the double-bitted axe and a unique specimen classed as a hoe.

In ground stone a roughly manufactured stone bowl is found. One sandstone abrader bears an irregular groove. In polished stone a solid atlatl weight with a grooved end is present.

In general, the distinction in artifact forms between the different periods is not marked. Changes to be noted are more pronounced in the changing popularity of styles than in the replacement or introduction of new forms. The emphasis during this entire period may have been placed, not on chipped- or ground-stone implements, but rather on perishable artifacts in basketry or wood. In the definition of Period B, it is possible that a small proportion of artifacts contemporary with Period A, or perhaps even antedating Period A as herein described, may be included. Such a possibility is, of course, suggested by the presence of the two points, similar to a Plainview type, which are included in Period B because of their presence in the lower section of the deposit at D1McVII. The total content of the lower half of the deposits at D1CaI and D1McVII, however, seems to be intermediary between the topmost levels of these sites and the deepest levels of site D1EvIII. The suggestion of the possible presence of earlier elements in Period B is advanced because the sites could have been occupied sporadically by early groups that left little in the way of cultural remains.

The nature of the differences between periods presents a problem in regard to the manner in which the importance of specific traits should be indicated. The conventional trait list, even when the absolute frequency of artifacts is given, tends to obscure some differences between components. Since the size of sites, as well as the areas excavated, varies, a high frequency at one site in comparison with a low frequency at another site does not necessarily indicate a varying importance of that implement at the two sites. We must also recognize that a simple tabulation of traits or implement types does not constitute a full analysis of that material. Utilizing the preceramic horizons described above as an example, the differences in frequency represent changes, not only in the popularity of particular styles of artifacts, but also changes in the basic subsistence and economic patterns of the horizons. The appearance and greater frequency of small projectile points in the later horizons suggests the possibility of introduction of the bow and arrow in contrast to the dominance of the spear thrower in the earlier periods. The relative abundance of projectile points indicates the importance of hunting in the complex. Stone scraping tools are thought to reflect the importance of skin dressing in the various horizons. Sandstone grinding tools similarly reflect an aspect of the subsistence patterns of the complex. There is a transition from a small, irregular grinding stone common in Period A, to a more abundant, carefully shaped mano in the succeeding periods. This trend may reflect either an increasing utilization of wild seeds or the introduction of agriculture. The type of grinding stone in periods B and C, the mano, is similar in size and form to that obviously used to grind corn in later agricultural horizons. Since corn is known to be present in Ozark Bluff-Dweller sites, it seems probable that the change in form of grinding stone found between Period A and periods B and C may indicate the adoption of maize horticulture. Other tools, however, indicating horticultural activities are not preserved. In regard to the manner in which these differences may be detected and quantitatively expressed, two methods are suggested. When operating within a specific category, scrapers or projectile points for example, the varying frequency of different types is probably best expressed as a simple percentage of the total number of artifacts in that category. To indicate the varying importance of scrapers or grinding stones, an index number rather than a percentage is probably more precise.

The nature of the percentage differences in projectile-point types is shown in Table VIII. The percentages are computed on the basis of the total number of points from that period in a given site. The correspondences in the percentages between different components of a single period, while generally similar, are not too close. The variability may be due to the fact that each period represents a long, but sporadic occupation, with cultural remains accumulating under different conditions at each site. A similar analysis of the scraper types is given in Table IX. Here, particularly, the percentages may be distorted by a low frequency at the sites. Were the frequencies higher, such an analysis might be more meaningful.

TABLE VIII

Percentage Differences in Frequency of Projectile-Point Types

Type	Period A	Period B			Period C	
	DlEvIII Zones A-C	EvIII	CaI	McVII	CaI	McVII
A1	1.9	2.8	16.3	7.1	12.6	10.9
A2	5.6	2.8	12.5	4.0	11.0	7.6
A3	1.9	..	1.9	4.0	3.0	1.8
B1	9.3	8.3	15.4	29.3	13.6	21.8
B2	7.4	47.2	8.7	14.1	13.1	20.9
B3	..	4.2	3.8	6.1	1.0	3.0
C	1.9	..	5.8	5.1	6.8	4.2
E1	59.3	12.5	16.3	7.1	11.0	4.5
E2	5.6	15.3	10.6	5.1	6.8	4.2
G1	..	..	..	..	7.3	3.6
G2	..	..	2.9	4.0	8.4	9.1
G3	..	..	..	8.1	2.1	7.3
H	5.6	2.8	..	2.0	.5	..
Plainview form	..	..	..	2.0	..	..
Unclassified	1.9	4.2	5.8	2.0	2.6	.9
Total number of points	54	72	104	99	191	330

TABLE IX

Percentage Differences in Frequency of Scraper Types

Scraper	Period A	Period B			Period C	
	DlEvIII Zones A-C	EvIII	CaI	McVII	CaI	McVII
Stemmed scraper	10.5	..	62.5	..	22.2	23.1
Side scraper	10.5	25.0	..	16.7	..	7.7
Type A scraper	..	..	25.0	16.7	16.7	3.8
Type B scraper	21.0	25.0	..	..	..	3.8
Type C scraper	26.3	50.0	12.5	33.2	38.9	26.9
Type D scraper	..	..	..	16.7	..	3.8
Type E scraper	31.5	25.0	..	16.7	..	26.9
Type F scraper	..	..	..	..	11.1	..
Concave-edge scraper	..	..	..	..	..	3.8
Scraper, unclassified	..	..	..	..	11.1	..
Total number of scrapers	19	5	8	6	18	26

If it is desirable to show the importance of chipped-stone scrapers, grinding stones, or other implements within a complex, it is suggested that an index number be utilized. If the frequency within a given site were expressed in terms of a percentage, the size of the percentage of any category obviously would be affected by the frequency of all the other categories. Thus, if the total number of projectile points in DlEvIII, Period A, were expressed in terms of a percentage of the total number of artifacts found in Period A of DlEvIII, it would be lower than a comparable percentage in any of the other periods. This would, in large part, be due to the fact that Period A of DlEvIII has a relatively large number of scrapers. Thus a percentage indicating the importance of hunting activities would be decreased by the tools relating to the skin dressing activity. This should really validate the importance of hunting, an activity which produced the skins in the first place. It is obvious that if we want to compare the relative importance of certain artifact categories, it must be done on a different basis. In all of the components the projectile points are a numerically important element of the artifact complex. The frequency of the projectile points may, therefore, be taken as a base and the frequency of the other artifact categories expressed as an index of this base. Utilizing this concept, we obtain the results given in Table X.

TABLE X

Indices of Artifact Types in Preceramic Periods

Artifact	Period A	Period B			Period C	
	DlEvIII Zones A-C	EvIII	CaI	McVII	CaI	McVII
Scrapers.	35.1	6.9	7.7	6.1	9.4	7.9
Large grinding stones	1.8	6.9	11.5	12.1	16.2	20.3
Small grinding stones	12.9	5.6	..	..	..	..
Chipped-stone drills .	3.3	1.4	1.0	7.1	6.3	3.3
Knives/core knives . .	74.1	72.2	32.7	32.3	23.5	20.9
Choppers.	20.3	20.8	..	1.0	..	.6

Table X is restricted to six artifact categories since other types occur at the sites in such small quantities that an index would probably not be significant. It is to be noted that, except for the chipped-stone drills, each of these categories shows marked differences in its index, a fact which appears to be indicative of evolutionary trends. Zone D of D1EvIII, classified as Period B, in several categories is much closer to the section of D1EvIII classified as Period A and may represent an intermediary phase between the two periods. A comparison of the indices indicates that the trends present are as follows: (1) scrapers are very important in Period A, declining in importance in periods B and C; (2) chipped stone knives are most important in Period A, decrease in importance in Period B, reaching a low in Period C; (3) choppers are important in Period A and only at site D1EvIII in Period B; (4) small grinding stones are important in Period A, decline in importance in Period B where they are present only in D1EvIII and are lacking in Period C; (5) large grinding stones, on the other hand, increase markedly in importance from Period A to Period C. The varying importance in grinding stones may indicate that while the grinding of small seeds is important in Period A, in the subsequent periods we find a larger grinding stone, of a size and shape normally associated with a maize-agriculture complex. Periods B and C may represent an agricultural horizon, while Period A represents an earlier stage in which hunting and gathering are the bases of the economy and skin dressing is more important.

B. RELATIONSHIPS TO OTHER OZARK COMPLEXES

Since we have defined our problem as an elucidation of the cultural and chronological position of the Ozark Bluff-Dweller culture, the first point to establish is the relationship of this culture to the Oklahoma components already described. Our basic knowledge of the Ozark Bluff-Dweller culture still rests upon the preliminary report published by Harrington (1924) though supplementary information on several points has been added by Gilmore (1930), Weltfish (1932), and Dellinger (1936). Cultural evidence indicates that hunting, fishing, and seed gathering were important, though horticulture was also practiced, since maize, beans, squash, gourds, and sunflowers were raised. Varied basketry remains, fur and feather robes, soft-soled moccasins, double-soled grass sandals, nets, cordage, and textiles have suggested an affiliation with the Southwest, while remains, such as birchbark buckets, suggest that other regions also have contributed to the complex. In the absence of stratigraphic information, however, one wonders whether this actually constitutes a single complex. Were horticulture and seed gathering equally important during the same period? Were moccasins and sandals both used during the same period? An even greater handicap, however, in making a comparison with the Oklahoma lithic components is that in the other preliminary descriptions attention has been focused on the perishable materials and little has been recorded concerning the stone artifacts. Since the Oklahoma sites are located in exposed areas, the inventory of artifacts is practically confined to stone artifacts, only a few of bone and shell being present.

From Harrington's statements, however, we can obtain a rough idea of the nature of the stone complex. In his 1924 paper he specifically mentioned the presence of manos and metates, the chipped-stone axe, rough scrapers, and hammerstones. Further, the stone complex is described as similar to that found at Jacobs Cavern (Peabody and Moorehead, 1904). Finally, Harrington stated that the points of Gypsum Cave type are found associated with the oldest culture which he excavated in the caves and rock shelters of the Ozarks in Arkansas and Missouri (Harrington, 1933:118). Though the specimens from Jacobs Cavern are useful in indicating the general nature of the Ozark Bluff-Dweller stone artifacts, they are not of value as far as period determination is concerned. Jacobs Cavern contained pottery, which would suggest that the cave contained a late occupation and, since no mention is made of the depth at which specimens were found, it is difficult to determine what belongs to the late component and what represents an earlier period. The stone implements, however, are generally similar to those present in the Oklahoma components. In projectile points, types A1 and A2 (Gypsum Cave type), B1 and B2, and E1 and E2 are present, according to the illustrations. In addition, perforators and bunts are mentioned while knives and scrapers appear to parallel Oklahoma forms. It is to be noted that in the Jacobs Cavern collection points with a tapering stem (Type A) constitute about 42 per cent of the total stemmed points.

The comparison of the contracting stem point of the Ozark region with the Gypsum Cave type is an interesting one. Since Harrington excavated both types, it would appear that we must accept his statement as implying that on the basis of form and flaking it is impossible to differentiate between the points of the two areas. Certainly, on the basis of illustrations they do seem similar. We may supplement these comparisons, however, by an examination of the size of the point in the two areas. Harrington (1933) has presented the precise dimensions of the Gypsum Cave points though the series is limited to eight examples. His measurements have been converted to millimeters in order to facilitate comparison. In length, the Gypsum Cave points range from 45 to 73 mm., the mean length being 52.9 mm. (lengths were estimated by Harrington, except for one unbroken specimen). In width they range from 19 to 30 mm., the mean width being 25.6 mm. Stem length ranges from 7 to 11 mm., the mean stem length being 8.6 mm. In form the Gypsum Cave points are comparable to Type A1 in the Oklahoma preceramic components. The mean length of Type A1 points in the various preceramic periods of the Oklahoma components ranges from 84 to 63.2 mm., the mean width from 36.7 to 32.8 mm., and the mean stem length from 16.3 to 20.7 mm. In all measurements, therefore, the Oklahoma points exceed the size of the Gypsum Cave points in a substantial amount. It is also to be noted that the larger dimensions fall in the earliest period of the Oklahoma components. An amplification of the utility of such an analysis of measurement in indicating relationships or differentiating between the points of distinct complexes is presented in Appendix II.

Though the information on the lithic artifact types of the Ozark Bluff-Dweller culture is not as ample as might be desired, it is suggestive from a comparative point of view. In the Oklahoma components chipped-stone axes are confined to Period C. Manos and metates are considered characteristic of periods B and C. While the large projectile-point types continue through all periods, Type B does not become important until Period B and, in particular, Period C. It would appear then, that periods B and C, as far as nonperishable artifacts are concerned, have the closest parallels with the Ozark Bluff-Dweller culture and in all probability represent the same culture. The equivalent of periods B and C, however, can not be distinguished as separate stages in the Ozark Bluff-Dweller material on the basis of present published material. The preceding Period A of the Oklahoma area may not even be represented in the Ozark Bluff-Dweller cultural remains. The beveled and serrated points and the ground base and stem are distinctive features and probably would have been mentioned or illustrated if they were present in the Ozark Bluff-Dweller sites. On the positive side, we do have in Period A the full-grooved axe which is specifically mentioned as absent in the Ozark Bluff-Dweller culture. In summary, periods B and C in the Oklahoma components appear to represent lithic complexes which are part of the same culture described as the Ozark Bluff-Dweller culture. Period A in the Oklahoma components appears to represent an earlier phase which has not been described as part of the Ozark Bluff-Dweller culture.

Other preceramic remains have been reported in the general area under consideration. In 1901 the attention of W. H. Holmes was drawn to a spring at Afton, Indian Territory (Ottawa County, Oklahoma, about six miles from the sites considered in this paper) which had produced both chipped-stone implements and fossil remains of the mammoth and mastodon. Holmes concluded that the site did not indicate the contemporaneity of human artifacts and the Pleistocene animals since the stone implements were in a localized section of a much larger stratum which contained the fossil remains. The site is nevertheless of interest in connection with the preceramic occupation of this region. Holmes collected more than 800 stone implements from the spring and estimated that originally it must have contained between 1,500 and 2,000. In addition, a small series of bone implements was recovered, but no traces of pottery are mentioned. While this deposit may represent an accumulation of implements or objects cast into the spring, as Holmes has suggested, the diversity of implements indicates that a cross section of the types utilized by the culture is present. In chipped stone Holmes mentioned projectile points, knives, unspecialized blades and roughed-out forms, and unshaped fragments. Bone implements include awls, antler flaking tools, and longitudinally split sections of antler which Holmes considers knife handles. The projectile points illustrated would fall almost entirely in types B1, B2, and B3 as described in the preceding section, with Type B3 having thick, squared barbs as the most common form. One of the distinctive blade shapes in the latter type (Holmes, 1903: Pls.12, 15), having a biconcave outline, is also present in Period B and is represented by two examples of Type A2 points at D1EvIII.

Earlier work of Harrington (1920), somewhat to the south of the Ozark Region, revealed a preceramic culture on the

Ouachita River near Hot Springs, Arkansas. On the north bank of the Ouachita between two small, lateral streams, Harrington tested a deep midden which revealed a stratified deposit. Pottery and small projectile points of his Caddoan complex were found in approximately the upper foot of the deposit. Below this, to a depth of 9 feet 9 inches, were found indications of a preceramic culture having large projectile points unlike those of the upper section. Harrington mentioned the presence of chips, rejects, broken blades, and thick, grooved "net-sinkers" in this lower section. Illustrations indicate the presence of projectile points of types B1, B2, E2, E1, and an unusual side-notched form. No points of Type A are illustrated. The only other artifact (indicated by illustration) from the deep deposit is a small piece of hematite.

The nearest parallel to the Oklahoma material is reported at site MAH in eastern Missouri near the city of Hannibal, only two miles from the Mississippi River (Eichenberger, 1944: 33-36). Nearly the full complement of projectile-point types of the Oklahoma preceramic components was found here, possibly even including the Plainview type. A numerically important group consists of small points of the Type G series. Unfortunately, the collection described was derived from surface finds so that the suggestion given by Eichenberger that the complex is a preceramic one requires verification. The similarities to the materials from the Oklahoma sites suggest a similar complex.

While many other early investigations were carried on in the caves and bluff shelters of the Ozark region, the descriptions given add little information to our knowledge of the preceramic period. These explorations were made largely in an attempt to find traces of early man in America. Since the result of this aspect of the investigation was negative, little attention appears to have been paid to the possibility of a sequential development in a more recent time period. Gerard Fowke, for example, found deposits of ash six and seven feet in thickness in several of the caves he excavated in central Missouri (Fowke, 1922: 28-34, 47-81). Pottery was found in these sites but it is not known whether it was distributed throughout the entire thickness of the deposit. Therefore, although the stone work shows many parallels to the preceramic horizon here discussed, the lack of control in the excavation procedures, or at least in the publication of such information, makes comparison impossible.

The survey of the preceramic remains of the Ozark region indicates that there are abundant materials which fall within this period. Though descriptions on the whole are inadequate, they nevertheless suggest a generally similar type of material. We may suggest that scattered groups possessing such a common cultural tradition once inhabited the Ozark Plateau. They first appeared during a prehorticultural stage and later adopted maize and other domesticated plants prior to the introduction of ceramics. Regional variants and temporal phases can only be determined through a precise analysis of artifact types which, at present, cannot be made on the basis of published material. The general nature of the horizon, however, is sufficiently well established to enable broader comparisons to be made in order to determine the basic affiliations of this area.

III. BROADER RELATIONSHIPS OF THE OZARK MATERIAL

In making broader comparisons of the known Ozark material we have noted two essentially different sets of data with which we may deal. First of all, there is the complex of stone implements from the Oklahoma components. On the basis of the evidence presented in the site descriptions, it seems evident that the implements all fall into a preceramic period and although the material was divided into three sequent periods, there is a definite continuity in the culture complex from the earliest to the latest period. The differences among the periods in terms of specific artifacts are essentially derived from the slow accretion of a few new elements and the changing popularity of some of the artifact types. This cultural change was interpreted as taking place partly because of a shifting economic base, that is, the change from a purely hunting and gathering economy to a limited use of horticulture.

The second set of data which we may use for comparative purposes is the long series of perishable items, recovered by Harrington and other workers, that formed the basis of the original description of the Ozark Bluff-Dweller culture. Though the basketry, clothing, wooden artifacts, and plant remains are potentially of great value in determining the cultural relationships of the area, several factors limit their use at the present time. Much of this material is not described in the detail necessary for precise statements of origin or relationships. Further, it is impossible to determine whether all this material is to be definitely regarded as part of a single cultural complex equivalent to the preceramic periods outlined above, or whether some of it may not be of later provenience. It seems essential, therefore, to make the basic comparisons by means of the stone complex and then to attempt to interpret the perishable materials in the light of the basic affiliations discovered through that aspect of the material culture.

In our search for comparable material, the field can be approximately delimited by a consideration of the rough temporal placement of the Ozark material and the general nature of the cultural complex. The superposition of pottery types on the occupation sites gives a terminal date of around A.D. 900-1200 for the preceramic complex, a dating dependent upon that given to the earliest appearance of Woodland pottery types in the region. The absence of pottery itself does not warrant an early placement of the complex since the Ozark region may well have lagged behind other areas in the adoption of this trait. The presence of only recent animals among the faunal remains and the relatively close similarity of the stone complex to that of later ceramic cultures in the area suggest that we are not dealing with a very early culture. Approximately one thousand years before and after the beginning of the Christian era, as cultures are commonly dated at the present time, seems a logical time span in which to make an intensive search for similar culture types. In this search we are primarily interested in discovering another nonceramic complex with a stronger development in chipped stone than in ground or polished stone and worked bone.

Though it may be an obvious point, it seems essential to stress that the important feature of a broad comparison is to discover the presence of an essentially similar complex rather than the presence of specific cultural traits held in common by two cultures. The comparisons must be in terms of specific items, but the object is to find a similar configuration of items. Because of the essentially simple nature of the artifact types in a nonceramic cultural complex utilizing principally stone artifacts, a comparative study of the distribution of individual items would lead one far afield both in time and space without yielding much information on cultural relations. In projectile points, for example, it has been noted that the contracting stem point (Type A) has been compared by Harrington with points of Gypsum Cave type, associated in Nevada with an early horizon contemporary with the extinct ground sloth (Harrington, 1933: 118). Type H points might be compared with the Paradise Pinto type (Amsden, 1937, Pl. XLIII F), which shows a marked similarity in general form and, like the Gypsum Cave type, dates from an early period. Other points of comparable age, also found beside former Pleistocene lakes in the Lake Mohave area, show coarse serrations similar to those found in the earliest period of the Ozark region as indicated by the Oklahoma components. Similarly, we may note the presence in the Ozark region of points of Plainview form comparable to those found in Texas in association with an extinct form of bison (Krieger, 1947). Such a comparison, while it might indicate diversity in ultimate origins if possibilities of convergence and survivals are ignored, would yield little information on immediate origins and cultural relationships. Essentially, such a procedure is like the comparative section in Harrington's original description of the Ozark Bluff-Dweller culture (Harrington, 1924), in which a list of traits shared with the southwestern tribes, northern and northeastern Algonkians, central Algonkians, and southern Siouans, Caddos, and Muskhogean, and surrounding tribes is given. While Harrington undoubtedly intended simply to indicate the diversity of the material composing this previously undescribed culture, if a listing of this sort were taken at its face value it would imply that the culture was a conglomerate of traits from different areas. Although such a picture might under certain conditions be true, it certainly should not be resorted to as an interpretation until the possibility of the derivation of the culture as a total complex from an antecedent culture is exhausted. Furthermore, it is essential that the complex be considered in terms of a cluster of specific types and forms. A generalized trait list of large projectile points, scrapers, knives, and other artifacts could be duplicated in nearly any region of the United States. Sweeping comparison on such a basis would be of little value.

Perhaps following the lead of Harrington in attributing a preponderance of the traits of the Ozark Bluff-Dweller culture to the Southwest, it has become almost a fashion in recent years to draw attention to the resemblances between the Ozark remains, as well as other early horizons in the East, and the

Southwestern Basket-Maker stage and in some instances to postulate that they are culturally related (Griffin, 1946: 43; Wedel, 1940: 304; Martin, Quimby, and Collier, 1947: 221, 337, 352). Such suggestions, for the most part, are made without a presentation of the evidence leading to the conclusions and need to be examined to determine to what extent the resemblances are deeper than the common possession of maize horticulture by nonceramic groups still relying to a considerable extent upon hunting and gathering techniques.

In making the basic comparison we are concerned with a Basket-Maker II or Basket-Maker culture as opposed to a later Modified-Basket-Maker period. Such an attempted comparison is definitely handicapped by the frequently noted sparsity of Basket-Maker chipped stonework (Kidder and Guernsey, 1921: 112; Kidder and Guernsey in Nusbaum, 1922: 124-25). It seems possible that this paucity of chipped-stone artifacts may represent a definite cultural feature rather than depend on the nature of the sites as suggested by Kidder and Guernsey. Normal habitation sites certainly have been excavated, and the scarcity of stone implements may in large part be due to the replacement of implements made of stone by types made of another material, or simply to the lack of stress in the cultural complex on stone implements. The chipped-stone artifacts present occur in a limited series of types including projectile points of several shapes. Though a large point with a diagonal corner notch is often spoken of as the typical Basket-Maker point, Kidder and Guernsey stated that "almost all our finished points are notched at right angles to the long axes" (Kidder and Guernsey, 1921: 87). In addition, they described a similar shape lacking notches, which is considered an unfinished point. A single point found in a Basket-Maker site in Utah has a straight base and shallow notch in the side. The forms parallel types B1 and B2 as described for the Ozark region. These types obviously represent but a small portion of the Ozark projectile-point assemblage.

Other chipped-stone artifacts present in the Basket-Maker complex also indicate the distinctness of the two cultures. Kidder and Guernsey described large knife blades over six inches in length having a stem produced by notches (Kidder and Guernsey, 1921: Pl. 35, J and K), a rare feature of the Ozark complex. Chipped-stone gravers represent one artifact of the southwestern Basket-Maker complex not found in the Ozark complex.

Kidder and Guernsey stated that the following traits are lacking, or at least have not been found in the Basket-Maker complex: grooved axes, chipped-stone scrapers, and long drills. The three items are present in the Ozark material, the last two in relative abundance and typological variety. Similar manos and grinding stones are held in common, but the wide distribution of these makes their mutual presence of little importance in determining cultural relationships. Other specific items tabulated as present in the trait lists of the Oklahoma preceramic periods add further weight to the cultural differences. In view of the scarcity of items held in common and the markedly different orientation of the stone complexes, it would appear from an examination of this aspect of the culture that the Basket-Maker and Ozark remains are basically unrelated complexes.

An elimination of the Basket-Maker culture does not, of course, rule out the possibility of southwestern affiliation. At a comparable time period and earlier both the Hohokam and Mogollon cultures had appeared as distinctive complexes, though they were already in a ceramic phase. Similarities which might be demonstrated in the lithic complex — the only aspect of the culture we need consider — may indicate a mutual derivation from a common culture. The Hohokam appears to be the easier to eliminate, since it consists of a highly specialized culture even in its lithic aspects. Even the early Pioneer period contains a variety of elaborate forms in ground and polished stone including stone vessels, palettes, three-quarter grooved axes, as well as mortars, pestles, hammerstones, anvils, and whetstones. Despite a later elaboration in chipped stone, particularly in ornate projectile points, the early period contains but a limited quantity of chipped-stone implements though apparently already containing a demarcation between small delicate points and larger dart points. The latter embrace but a limited series of forms though the feature of a serrated body might be noted with the dominant type being comparable to Type A1. Drills, crude scrapers, and hand axes (choppers ?) are present in small quantities (Gladwin, and others, 1937). The resemblances of this complex as a whole to the Ozark region are quite limited, very few traits being held in common.

The early material from the Mogollon complex, that of the Hilltop (Haury, 1947), Pine Lawn (Martin, 1940, 1943, and 1947), and Penasco phases (Sayles, 1945), deserves more careful consideration. Aside from presenting comparative material in the proper time period, it also serves to give some indication of possible connections with the earlier Cochise culture from which the lithic elements of the Mogollon complex are thought to be derived. The latter aspect is an important one since the available descriptions of Cochise can provide us with only a limited series of artifacts, particularly in chipped stone (Sayles and Antevs, 1941). The sampling imposed by the nature of the sites may unduly shorten the inventory of implements for Cochise, and the greater variety in early Mogollon may, then, indicate forms that will be recorded in the Cochise complex when additional excavation is carried on. The lithic content of the three early phases of Mogollon are not identical but show some regional variation. In general, however, as far as ground stone is concerned there is a variety of tools for the treatment of both wild seeds and corn — manos of varied shapes, rubbing stones, pestles, mortars, and metates. In addition, paint palettes, pitted pebbles, full-grooved and three-quarter grooved mauls and tubular pipes are present. We may note that chipped stone is not only more varied but more abundant than in other southwestern cultures. To make specific comparisons with the Ozark region, forms comparable to types B1, B2, and E2 are most common in the Pine Lawn Phase. The Hilltop Phase, on the other hand, contains a greater number of leaf-shaped points with only a slight shoulder demarcating the stem. These points have some resemblances to types A3 and E1. Points generally similar to types C and G are also noted in limited quantities and, in addition, small delicate points are present. Scrapers are primarily found in the form of slightly modified flakes, but serrate and ground-edge scrapers may be listed as specialized forms. Drills are present, particularly in the Hilltop Phase, the shapes including T-shaped and needle-like forms. Gravers and choppers are abundant.

There are clearly a great many more traits held in common between Mogollon and the Ozark region than can be demonstrated for any of the other southwestern complexes. Despite these similarities, even without considering the total complex of houses, pottery, bone, and other items, it is obvious that there is considerable divergence in the lithic elements. The presence of mauls, palettes and pipes in Mogollon and the absence of full-grooved axes are but a few of the factors which show the distinctness of the two cultures. Obviously we cannot derive the

Ozark complex from Mogollon, but if those same resemblances could be traced back to an earlier culture such as Cochise, we might consider the possibility of that culture affecting eastern complexes at an early period. This, however, must remain as a possible problem for future archaeological work, since it cannot be demonstrated at the present time.

On the northern periphery of the southwestern area early cultures that are the equivalent in time to the Basket-Maker period or earlier are not known in any degree of completeness but are based primarily on a few projectile-point types. Including the High Plains region, the chief landmark in the early preceramic cultures that are adequately defined is Signal Butte I. Strong (1935: 224-39) has characterized Signal Butte I as being primarily a chipped-stone culture though a few ground-stone implement types including grinding stones, shaft polishers, grooved mauls, and an axe with ground notches are present. The chipped-stone industry is particularly characterized by the use of flakes with excellent retouching. Plano-convex scrapers are abundant as are several types of projectile points. Sixty-five per cent of all the projectile points consist of a leaf-shaped or lanceolate form. Twenty-eight per cent are stemmed points (SCa2, SCa3 and SCb3 according to Strong's classification), which parallel types B1 and B3 in shape though they are considerably smaller. An additional form present in limited quantities is a small point that has basal and horizontal side notches. Aside from the differences in form, the fact that many of the points are unifaced retouched flakes indicates the distinctiveness of the culture from the Ozark remains. Three types of scrapers are described, including an end scraper retouched on a thick flake, an end scraper with the dorsal surface retouched to form a definite keel, and a third type having a definite stem, though these are not the modified projectile-point forms that constitute the stemmed scrapers of the Ozark region. Other scraper forms include ovoid side scrapers and spokeshaves (concave edge). Chipped-stone drills and gravers are present, the drills having a more irregular basal area than is characteristic of the Ozark region at the early period. Even with this limitation of the discussion to the stone complex, it is evident that Signal Butte I has little in common with the preceramic complex of the Ozark region but has, on the one hand, a marked similarity to certain features of the early hunting cultures, and on the other, a distinct specialization in another direction. Subsequent levels at Signal Butte show further developments of this specialization in artifact types. Signal Butte II is also a preceramic culture but here the proportions of the various projectile points are reversed in comparison with Signal Butte I. In Signal Butte II, 61 per cent of all the projectile points are stemmed points, both with and without barbs (Scb2 and SCa2 according to Strong's classification). Leaf-shaped points become a minority type. Other characteristic chipped-stone implements include abundant side scrapers, end scrapers, drills, and gravers. The drills include a T-shaped form, quite similar to that of the Ozark region, and the projectile-point complex also exhibits a greater similarity to the Ozark projectile-point complex than is shown by Signal Butte I. At present Signal Butte II is characterized by a much more restricted series of artifact types than is found in the Ozark region. Though it is possible that further excavations may amplify this list, Signal Butte II gives the impression of being an earlier, less elaborate culture complex.

On the southern and eastern margins of the southwestern area, the early preceramic cultures that have been briefly described in the west Texas area might be expected to show a greater resemblance to the Ozark area. But the Clear Fork and Round Rock foci, as presented in the recent summary description of Kelley (1947), lack the richness in cultural content on which an evaluation of similarity could be based. The Clear Fork Focus includes in its inventory of stone implements, end and side scrapers, spokeshaves, gravers, hand axes, discs, and abrading stones. Four types of dart points are considered diagnostic. Two of these, Baird Beveled Blade and Taylor Thinned Base, to use Kelley's terminology, are basically triangular forms which are absent in the Ozark region. The remaining two, Pedernales Indented Base and Nolan Beveled Stem, though in general shape perhaps similar to types E1 and E2, possess distinctive features such as the beveled stem and deeply indented base on a parallel-sided stem that are not characteristic of the Ozark region. The similarities, however, may be greater than suggested in the above discussion. Krieger (1946: 118) illustrates a series of dart points from the M. D. Harrell site, a Henrietta Focus component, which are described as common types in Edwards Plateau nonceramic cultures that appear to have survived into the Henrietta Focus complex. These include good examples of types B2, E2, and perhaps H, as they are classified for the Ozark region. Beveled-blade forms are also present. It is evident, however, that the complete, or even reasonably full, assemblage of Ozark chipped-stone implements is not to be duplicated as an assemblage and that the stress, in terms of popularity, rests on different forms.

In the absence then of any indications of strong cultural ties with the western and southwestern cultures, we may turn our attention to the material found in the East and Southeast. On the basis of plant remains Jones (1936: 162) stressed the great similarity between material found in the caves of Kentucky and the Ozark Bluff-Dweller material. Jones stated that the similarities are marked in the textiles, local cultivated plants, and wild food plants, and said further (1936: 164) that "there is almost nothing in the Newt Kash material which cannot be duplicated from the Ozarks." In the Kentucky sites remains of Iva, Chenopodium, Ambrosia, and Helianthus (sunflower) occur in an apparently precorn as well as prepottery level. These same plants occur in the Ozark region, though the list of material is more varied, particularly in cultivated plants.

The artifactual material from Newt Kash shelter in Menifee County, Kentucky, the site upon which the statements of Jones on plant remains are based, is not described in detail. The illustrations of projectile points (Webb and Funkhouser, 1936: Figure 16) do indicate, however, that nearly all of the projectile points of large size characteristic of the Oklahoma components are present. The only exceptions to this appear to be Type A3, Type H, and the Plainview form. The presence here of a similar range in shapes common to the two areas is in striking contrast to the extremely spotty resemblances that can be seen when the Ozark complex is compared with sites located to the west of the Ozark region. Similar knives and possibly also scrapers are present though the nature of the illustrations does not permit precise comparisons in the latter category. In ground and polished stone, hoes, grooved plummets, and fragments of gorgets are present. Though these implements are lacking in the Oklahoma components, the hoes were noted as present by Harrington in the Ozark Bluff-Dweller culture, and the grooved plummet was present in the preceramic complex found by Harrington near Hot Springs, Arkansas. Other bluff shelters in the same general area of east-central Kentucky contain additional artifacts that are probably also a part of the Kentucky complex and parallel the Oklahoma specimens. Big Ash Cave in Lee County, Kentucky (Funkhouser and Webb, 1929), adds chipped-stone drills and the full-grooved axe to the list of stone artifacts. The similarity of textile remains from this site and Newt Kash shelter suggests that the two Kentucky sites, as well as many others in this general area, represent a single complex. Any ultimate determination of degree of relationship between the Kentucky material and the Ozark Bluff-Dweller culture will probably rest on these same textile remains. Jones' statement on the similarity of textiles (Jones, 1936: 164) appears to be based on the similarity of materials utilized rather than upon a similarity of techniques. The great diversity of basketry techniques present in the Ozark material which cannot be duplicated in published reports on Kentucky suggests a marked divergence in cultural complexes. The form of footgear, frequently designated a sandal though resembling a slipper, found in the Kentucky area and lacking in the Ozarks, is a good case in point. In Kentucky the mano of the Ozark region is replaced by a pestle. The Kentucky sites also appear to contain a greater variety of both bone and polished stone implements, although the latter do not appear to be present in large quantities and their chronological position is not clear.

Despite the differences mentioned above, the two cultural complexes appear to have much in common. The similarities might be accentuated by a clearer chronological picture in both areas. This marked similarity, however, may well be due to a common origin in, or influence from, a third culture, the eastern Archaic. Indeed, it has been suggested that there is no distinctive occupation in the Kentucky shelters, but that these shelters have been occupied sporadically by various cultural groups, chief among these being the Archaic.

In considering relationships with the Archaic horizon we are, of course, not limited to comparison with the Archaic sites of Kentucky alone, since the presence of the horizon has been demonstrated throughout nearly all of the eastern United States, primarily east of the Mississippi River. An interjection of temporal depth in the Archaic of Tennessee and Alabama, the first region for which this was achieved in the Southeast, was initially given by the descriptions of the deep shell mounds containing a lower zone of predominantly bone implements, worked flint appearing as a later trait (Webb and DeJarnette, 1942: 306-19). This sequential development in the Archaic has since been presented in a more precise form with three distinct prepottery periods of the Archaic defined (Webb and DeJarnette, 1948). The periods are numbered, Archaic 1 being the earliest.

The artifactual content of Archaic 1, as at present defined, is extremely limited. Double-pointed bone projectile points, split bone awls, and antler shaft straighteners comprise the total list (Webb and DeJarnette, 1948: 18). Though the absence of worked flint is specifically mentioned, it is difficult to conceive how such a culture could function without it. Abundant cut and worked bone are mentioned, but an elucidation of the techniques of manufacturing these bone implements is needed, since common techniques of manufacturing such implements imply the use of chipped-stone tools or at least of stone flakes. Furthermore, it is difficult to see how a culture, in part relying on hunting, could function without the use of stone knives.

The implements and other traits of the Archaic 1 period continue through the subsequent Archaic 2 period, which is characterized by the addition of new traits rather than by the disappearance of old ones. Flintwork suddenly becomes abundant. The stone implement types described as characteristic of the period are those earlier presented in the Pickwick Basin report (Webb and DeJarnette, 1942). Though we have no reason to doubt the validity and utility of these typological divisions, it is unfortunate that illustrations are the chief source of information on their form and variation. Illustrations used to determine form, show that the chipped-stone types of Archaic 2 consist of leaf-shaped blades with one end pointed and the base either rounded or straight, and elongated ovate blades with one end slightly pointed. The characteristic projectile points have a straight-sided or expanding stem, though a lanceolate and a side-notched form are also present. The chipped-stone implements also include drills, both in a form gradually expanding to the base, and as a modified projectile point. Ground-stone implements include hammerstones and bell-shaped pestles.

Archaic 3 is marked by a changing popularity in chipped-stone implements. The dominant projectile points of this period include a contracting stem form, a type having a parallel-sided stem which is proportionately long and narrow, and a type having a broad flaring stem. The period is also marked by the appearance of a number of artifacts of polished stone, including gorgets and atlatl weights. The presence of carved stone bowls is also a characteristic feature of the period.

We have limited the discussion of this period sequence primarily to stone artifacts since any comparison with the Ozark region must be based on that complex; the period distinctions, however, are also marked in other aspects of the culture, including bone implements and burial types. In regard to projectile points, it is interesting to note that the Archaic 2 period appears to contain a large proportion of points that would be comparable to Type E, whereas the Archaic 3 period appears to contain a large proportion of Type A points. This trend parallels the one noted in the Oklahoma sites where Type E is also more important in the earliest of the preceramic periods. The period breakdown does not do justice to the remarkably close correspondence in the lithic complex of the two areas, since many of the types present in smaller quantities are not included. An inspection of the illustrations of projectile points reveals no forms lacking that are present in the Ozark region. It might be specifically mentioned that this also includes points of the Plainview form as represented in the Ozark region (Webb and DeJarnette, 1942: Pl. 226). We find a similar situation in regard to the forms of drills and knives and in the presence of the full-grooved axe. The relative abundance of these artifacts may vary widely, however, and we have no information on scraper types and the forms of abraders. A specific difference which may be noted is the utilization of the pestle in Tennessee rather than either the mano or a small, flat grinding stone.

An examination of the illustrations in the report on the Eva Focus in western Tennessee (Lewis and Kneberg, 1947), however, indicates that some of the traits which could not be specifically noted as present in the other reports considered are definitely present in the Archaic of Tennessee. A variety of scrapers are illustrated including the stemmed scraper. Very specific parallels are to be remarked in the projectile points, since both beveled and serrated blades are present as in the early period of the Ozark region. With the exception of the double-bitted axe, which appears late in the Oklahoma sequence, and possibly choppers, all of the chipped-stone implements seem to be duplicated. The typical grinding stone, however, still appears to be the pestle. It might be noted that in the recently described Archaic site in Illinois, the Faulkner site, grinding stones similar to the Oklahoma components are present (MacNeish, 1948).

In the Ozark region the absence of many of the typical artifacts in both polished stone and bone indicates that we are not dealing with the simple extension of an early Archaic horizon. The similarities do suggest, however, that the material is generically related to it. It seems unlikely that all of the regional variants of the Archaic have been defined, and probably some of the westerly variants may be closer to the Ozark complex. There is perhaps a suggestion of a difference between the eastern and western extensions of the complex in the form of stone used in grinding seeds; a flat grinding stone is used in the west and a pestle is used in the east. Perforated atlatl weights seem more common toward the east, while boatstones are more common toward the west. Even on the basis of the present evidence the Ozark complex appears to have more in common with the Archaic than with any of the other complexes discussed. In spite of the spatial gap between the specific manifestations discussed, it seems possible that this indication of relationship will be strengthened when the archaeology of the intervening area is better known.

Turning from this consideration of the location of a similar complex of stone implements which indicates the relationships of the Ozark complex, we may consider some of the specific items of culture found in the Ozark region, including the perishable remains, to see what light they throw on the affiliations of the culture. In perishable materials the artifacts again differ from the Basket-Maker complex proper, though they show some similarities to the greater Southwest.

A small selection of the coiled basketry of the Ozark region has been examined and described by Weltfish (1932: 114). The foundation utilized was both two-rod-vertical and single-rod which contrasts with the typical Basket-Maker two-rod-and-bundle-triangular foundation, two-rod-and-reed-triangular foundation (Weltfish, 1932: 109). The two-rod-vertical foundation was combined with stitches split on the nonwork surface, probably a concave work surface, and the single-rod foundation has interlocking stitches. Both types show a left direction of work and a plaited starting knot. Though Weltfish (1932:109) had considered the single-rod foundation with interlocking stitches as possibly intrusive in the Southwest, Morris and Burgh (1941: 7) described baskets with a single-rod foundation and interlocking stitches as present in Basket Maker III, Pueblo I and III periods. The Ozark material is mentioned as being paralleled in modern work in the coiled gambling baskets of the Paviotso, Shoshoni, and Plains tribes (Weltfish, 1932: 117). Further examination of the basketry remains of the Ozark region, however, would probably reveal a greater variety of coiled types. In a somewhat neglected paper of D. I. Bushnell, Jr. (1905: 319), a fragmentary basket found in the southern part of McDonald County, Missouri, is described as having a grass foundation. The foundation type is interesting since a survey of its distribution indicates that a grass-bundle foundation is prevalent in western Texas and in Coahuila, Mexico (Cosgrove, 1947: 110). A detailed description of other perishable materials of the Ozark Bluff Dwellers is available only for the baby cradles (Dellinger, 1936). Several types are present. A flexible form is described as similar to Basket-Maker material described for northeastern Arizona (Dellinger, 1936: 210; Kidder and Guernsey, 1919: 165-66). Dellinger stated (1932: 213), however, that possibly only the rigid types are to be assigned to the Ozark Bluff Dwellers, so that the flexible type may represent the form present in the later Top Layer culture. The rigid types are comparable to those seen in the Great Basin among the Paviotso, Shivwits, and Moapa (Dellinger, 1932: 214). Thus, while some traits in basketry materials are held in common with the Southwest, they do not clearly point to affiliations with a Basket-Maker horizon. As in the list of southwestern traits presented by Harrington (1924: 14-15), many are of wider occurrence and some are more characteristic of later horizons.

It is this common presence of basketry forms which probably has been the basis of some of the broader comparisons of the Ozark region with the Southwest. The origin of the basketry types and their routes of diffusion would therefore be of crucial importance in determining the source of some of these influences in the Ozark complex. One hypothesis of southwestern cultural development, most clearly presented by Steward (1940: 452-53, 460-62), suggests that the Basket-Maker culture represents a period when basketry and perhaps some hunting techniques were introduced into the Southwest. Basketry, therefore, is considered to be of a relatively recent introduction and further to involve population expansion and probably migration. If this concept of a recent introduction and spread of basketry as a trait accompanying migration is accepted, it provides a strong point for suggesting a relationship between the Ozark remains and the Southwest.

Steward stated that the source of the basketry complex

remains in doubt. Though a West Coast origin, first for coiled and later for twined basketry, has been the general interpretation, Steward (1940:453), surveying recent evidence of coiled basketry in Middle and South America, suggested that a Middle American or Mexican source for Basket-Maker basketry is not impossible. His hypothesis provides a means of accounting for the basketry complex in the Ozark region without resorting to southwestern affiliation or origin. Both the Ozark region and the Southwest may have obtained the basketry from a common source. A suggestion of a wider distribution of coiled basketry in the Southeast than previously has been considered is perhaps indicated by basket imprints on pottery.

The basket imprints on pottery deserve further consideration since Griffin's analysis of this material may indicate why he has considered the two areas, as well as others, to represent a similar stage and to be culturally related. He noted (1946:44-45) that "the appearance of basketry impressions on early Basketmaker pottery is paralleled by the appearance of basket-marked pottery in Osark Bluff-Dweller sites and in related sites in southwestern Arkansas, at Stalling's Island, in east Tennessee, in New Jersey, in other early levels in the Mississippi Valley, in southwestern Alaska, in Mexico, and in eastern Brazil."

Aside from the common possession of a form of surface modification, these wares, upon closer analysis, do not appear to be comparable. The mutual presence of basketry impressions may well be the result of quite distinct functional causes. In the Southwest the presence of basket impressions on pottery, appearing early in Basket-Maker pottery and surviving in many later horizons, seems clearly the result of a constructional process involving the molding of the lower part of the vessel within a basket or using a basket to support the moist, flexible walls. The pottery to be found at Stalling's Island may, it is true, have developed in a similar manner. Published illustrations of the pottery suggest, however, that basket-like impressions are used in this complex primarily as a decorative device (Claflin, 1931: Pls. 12, 13, 18). In many cases the pottery bears not an actual basket impression, but a stamped or punctate decoration simulating basket impressions. In confirmation of this point the vessels illustrated by Martin, Quimby, and Collier

(1947:372, Figure 93) are an excellent example of a skeuomorph. These vessels imitate a coiled basket in form as well as in surface appearance. The Ozark Bluff-Dweller sites illustrate another distinct type. Basket impressions are normally confined to the base of the vessel. It may be that in this area the baskets were used simply as a rest for the pot, a variety of tournette, to facilitate the construction of the vessel. The basketry impressions in this instance appear to be largely accidental impressions that were not desired for their decorative effect as is suggested particularly in the Stalling's Island complex and perhaps in the Southwest as well. In addition, the construction technique is different from that indicated in the Southwest. It is further to be questioned whether the Ozark Bluff-Dweller pottery is to be considered an early manifestation of pottery. At present it is impossible to isolate a specific pottery type that can be said to represent the closing phases of this complex, nor is it possible to demonstrate that the pottery has an antiquity in any way comparable to that assigned to the Ozark Bluff-Dweller culture. The basket-impressed forms described by Dellinger and Dickinson (1942) have their closest parallel to wares that in Oklahoma are to be found in Fourche Maline Focus sites (Newkumet, 1940), and even in Spiro Focus sites (Baerreis, 1947: 4-5). In general, the pottery described by Dellinger and Dickinson for the Ozark Bluff Dwellers seems to be a mixture of a number of types from different cultures. The wares suggest that the shelters subsequent to the Ozark Bluff-Dweller occupation were occupied sporadically by many different peoples over a fairly long time period, though for relatively short intervals. In short, a greater antiquity than the Marksville horizon remains to be demonstrated for the pottery types represented in the sherds of Dellinger and Dickinson. Also to be proved is the relationship of the pottery to the Ozark Bluff-Dweller culture.

The functional distinctions suggested above in regard to the basket impressions on pottery in some of the areas cited by Griffin indicate that it is not possible in all instances to equate this pottery without a more thorough investigation. Though surface malleations on pottery may be an old and important trait, all basket impressions are definitely not to be considered in this category nor even thought to indicate a single, related trait. The wide distribution, however, of basketry impressions adds further weight to the suggestion that in the eastern half of the

United States we should not depend upon an introduction and spread of basketry from a southwestern Basket-Maker horizon. It may, indeed, be far older in the Southwest itself. Though basketry is not known for the Cochise culture, the abundant grinding stones as well as the total cultural content suggest a cultural complex strikingly similar to that of the later Basket-Maker and Intermontane peoples. If Steward (1940: 452) is correct in suggesting that such a mode of life would be difficult without, among other traits, the basket types essential for seed gathering, the apparent absence of baskets in the culture may simply be the result of poor conditions of preservation. Basketry may, then, have diffused at a much earlier time period. A further point to be mentioned in this connection is that among the basketry types of the Ozark Bluff-Dweller culture, Harrington mentioned one that resembles the twined weave of the contemporary Paiute water bottles. Since twined basketry is not present in the Basket-Maker horizon, either this must represent a trait which diffused only recently or it must be considered as supplementary evidence for a southern origin or point of entry for the basketry complex, with the latter appearing more probable.

An important factor in considering the relationships of the Ozark culture is the presence of maize in several varieties which are also found in the Southwest. If it were possible to accept Carter's hypothesis regarding the spread of these varieties of corn from the East to the Southwest, this factor would not need to be considered as indicating southwestern affiliation. In the light of the extremely critical reviews (Jones, 1946; Willey, 1946; Haury, 1946) pointing out the mass of evidence contrary to such a view, it hardly seems necessary to consider such a possibility.

In reviewing the current status of corn research, Volney H. Jones stated (1949) that in the East only two types of corn differ from the dominant eastern complex. One of the types is similar to the Basket-Maker corn of the Southwest and was found at Ozark Bluff-Dweller sites and at Canter's Cave shelter in Ohio. The second type appears to be a more dilute form of another variety derived from the Southwest, which was present at sites in Kentucky, Illinois, and the Missouri river drainage at a somewhat later time period. The history of the Hohokam-Basket-Maker corn complex, that present in the Ozark area, is summarized by Jones (1949: 246) as follows:

This complex appears to have been the earliest in areas north of Mexico. It has its affiliations in the Sierra Madre Occidental, whence it moved into the Hohokam area at least as early as 200 to 100 B.C. It persisted as the only type in Hohokam archaeology and, to historic times, as the sole type in the agriculture of the Pima, Papago, and the Yuman tribes of the lower Colorado.

It appeared in Basketmaker context in the San Juan area by about 200 A.D. as the earliest type in Anasazi agriculture. It was absorbed by the Mexican Complex, which entered in late Basketmaker or early Pueblo times. The replacement was complete in most of the area, but a few Hopi varieties contain influence of the former strain.

It spread through the Prairie area and reached the Ozark Bluff Dwellings by about 500 to 600 A.D., apparently as the earliest type, and moved on to the Ohio rock shelters. In the Prairie this complex mixed first with the Mexican Complex and later with the Eastern Complex. In the East it was absorbed by the Eastern Complex.

Though this would suggest southwestern affiliation for a part of the Ozark culture complex, the distributional data is not sufficiently abundant to make it certain that the Basket-Maker complex is the sole possible source for the variety of corn in the Ozark region. Both the Ozark area and the Southwest may have received the corn from northern Mexico without all corn of this type traveling eastward by way of the Southwest. Whatever its ultimate origin, whether from the Southwest or directly from the higher cultures to the south, its presence does not immediately suggest total cultural derivation or the derivation of even a sizeable complex of traits from the Southwest. The diffusion of corn does not appear to have been accompanied by a large body of affiliated traits.

The discussion of perishable material briefly entered into above throws little light on the origin and growth of the Ozark complex. Both descriptions and distributional evidence at the present time seem inadequate for sound conclusions. It is possible, however, that the last phase of the preceramic period is marked by the accretion of a number of elements from varied sources, some perhaps derived from the Southwest, some from other sources. The single polished stone atlatl weight found in Level 3 of site DlMcVII is one item in the latter category. Its provenience suggests that it represents an element of Period C, the most recent of the preceramic periods. Excavations in the Southeast have given some indication of the development of this form of atlatl weight, commonly designated a boatstone. The boatstones of the Tchefuncte culture are crude, solid forms having oval or elongated oval outlines and are plano-convex in cross section. Fine grooves are mentioned as being present on the ends (Ford and Quimby, 1945: 37-39). The boatstones of the next successive culture, Marksville, are commonly thinner, elongated forms which are much more carefully manufactured and possess a distinct keel, an interior cavity, and frequently bear perforations (Ford and Willey, 1940: 106-8). In this sequence of forms, therefore, the boatstone of Period C resembles the Tchefuncte forms, though it is somewhat more carefully finished. This would appear to be an element derived from cultures developing to the south and east of the Ozark region.

In the preceding section, we have also indicated that one method of characterizing a cultural complex is to present by means of an index the relative frequency of certain artifact forms. Both as a means of testing the utility of such a concept and to further test our suggested relationships, we may examine similar indices for Archaic sites. In Table XI the frequency and indices of certain artifact forms for a series of sites classed as Archaic is presented. The high index of scrapers indicates a similarity to Period A in the Oklahoma components of the Ozark Bluff-Dweller culture. The indices may not seem very close when those of Table XI are compared with Table X, but it must be considered that if similar indices for southwestern sites were computed, the affinities of the Oklahoma components to the eastern Archaic would be more pronounced. The extremely small number of chipped-stone implements reported in most publications dealing with the Southwest, however, make such comparisons impractical.

Aside from any potential value in comparative studies that such indices may have, they are useful in indicating the importance of a particular artifact category at a particular site. MacNeish, for example, specifically mentioned the "numerous grinding and pounding implements" at the Faulkner site, yet Table VIII indicates that, compared to other eastern Archaic components, the frequency is remarkably low.

In the light of the total comparisons with other areas, it was felt that the strongest affiliations of the Ozark material were to be found in the eastern Archaic. This conclusion was specifically derived from a study of the distribution of lithic complexes. A discussion of the perishable items did not strengthen this conclusion, but it was evident that present evidence does not

TABLE XI

Frequency and Indices of Certain Artifact Categories in Archaic Sites

	Artifact	Site 1	2	3	4	5
Frequency	Projectile points	253	253	54	300	69
	Knives/blades	22	14	2	111	26
	Drills	64	38	10	149	10
	Scrapers	178	195	46	331	113
	Pestles	58	55	5	122	
	Manos					2
Indices	Knives/blades	8.7	5.5	3.7	37.0	37.6
	Drills	25.3	15.1	18.5	49.6	14.5
	Scrapers	70.3	77.4	85.1	110.3	168.2
	Pestles	22.9	21.8	8.3	40.6	
	Manos					3.0

1. Site 4, McLean County, Kentucky (Webb and Haag, 1947)
2. Site 7, McLean County, Kentucky (Webb and Haag, 1947)
3. Site 8, McLean County, Kentucky (Webb and Haag, 1947)
4. Chiggerville Site 1, Ohio County, Kentucky (Webb and Haag, 1939)
5. Faulkner Site, Illinois (MacNeish, 1948)

require an interpretation deriving this material in its totality from the Southwest. Indications of temporal depth in the Archaic suggest that at an early period this culture was primarily dependent upon bone implements. The later emphasis on chipped-stone work may be a result of the diffusion of a possible late Cochise phase which would account for some general resemblances between the Southwest and Southeast, if it were accompanied by perishable artifacts including basketry, which is not represented in the open sites because of unfavorable conditions of perservation. Comparisons made specifically with a Basket-Maker horizon appear to be aimed at a culture which is both somewhat late in time and too specialized in its own direction to serve as a point of origin for the resemblances.

IV. SUMMARY AND CONCLUSIONS

In the preceding sections the problem of temporal change within the Ozark Bluff-Dweller culture has been attacked through a series of preceramic sites in Delaware County, northeastern Oklahoma. It has been possible to postulate objectively three sequent periods in the development of the preceramic culture. These periods are considered to parallel, in part at least, the Ozark Bluff-Dweller culture and to be the local manifestation of that culture. Since these are open sites, they lack perishable materials. A clear cultural continuity is seen in the three periods defined, the period distinctions apparently in large part resulting from a shifting economic base. Since it is possible that all of the perishable materials, which to date have formed the basis of the description of the Ozark Bluff-Dweller culture, do not constitute a single cultural complex, the specific relationships of these data to the three periods are not clear. It is, therefore, suggested that the Oklahoma preceramic complex be designated the Grove Focus. Since the Grove Focus does provide a sequential framework and its temporal position is at least fixed in its terminal date as prior to the Woodland ceramic penetration into this area, the perishable materials can then be worked into this framework with additional detailed stratigraphic information and study.

A comparative study of this complex with those of other regions has indicated that specific affiliations of the culture lie with the Southeast rather than with the Southwest, though influences from the Southwest are still a strong possibility. The attempt to make broad comparisons has indicated that descriptive detail for many of the common artifact categories, such as projectile points and scrapers, as presented in current reports is not adequate for the precise determination of cultural origins and relationships. A general similarity of some aspects of the Ozark material to other preceramic cultures, such as the southwestern Basket-Maker culture, remains as a fact. It seems possible to explain this similarity on other than the grounds of cultural affiliation. In both regions horticulture was introduced to hunting and gathering peoples who lacked ceramics as a means of producing containers. A similar elaboration in containers of basketwork might be expected to develop under the increasing need of containers for seed storage. Similar robes and footgear may well represent an old trait, widely diffused in the course of a long period of time. Extremely favorable conditions of preservation could then give an impression of relationship which would not be felt were the distributional data better understood. Despite a broad comparative study, no clear account has been given to show what an old "Basket-Maker-like" culture consists of, nor to prove that such a complex is present over this broad area.

Further interpretation might be made on a more speculative level, going beyond the limits of the conclusions that may be supported by the data presented in this paper. The Eastern Archaic would appear to represent a cultural complex which has received substantial increments of traits from diverse sources. A dominant cultural strain at an early period consists of a cultural complex having an emphasis on its bone industry, this being suggested by the Archaic 1 period as defined in the Alabama—Tennessee area. There is a possibility of an Asiatic origin for such a culture complex since the presence of a similar culture to the north is suggested by the Lamoka Focus in New York, which has a similar emphasis on bone work (Ritchie, 1944: 321). It is in the succeeding Archaic 2 period that an important lithic complex is added to the earlier bone industry. Marked parallels are to be found between the early periods in the Ozark region and the Eastern Archaic in this same lithic complex. The absence of the elaborations in the bone industry in the Ozark region suggests that the lithic complex may have diffused separately. The Faulkner site in Illinois is perhaps an indication that in the western margin of the eastern archaeological province the basic Archaic culture consists of this predominantly lithic complex. In the Ozark region a ready means of communication with the western United States is provided by the river systems which flow eastward and southeastward to touch upon the southern extensions of the Ozarks. Additional elements may have been added to the Eastern Archaic, while at the same time some portions of the complex spread westward.

In general, there is at present a real need for the further study and redescription of older collections in the light of new problems that have been formulated since the early excavations were made, as well as for further excavations with specific problems in view. If such studies are designed to test and develop hypotheses of culture growth and elaboration, we may expect significant progress in the interpretation of the archaeology of the United States.

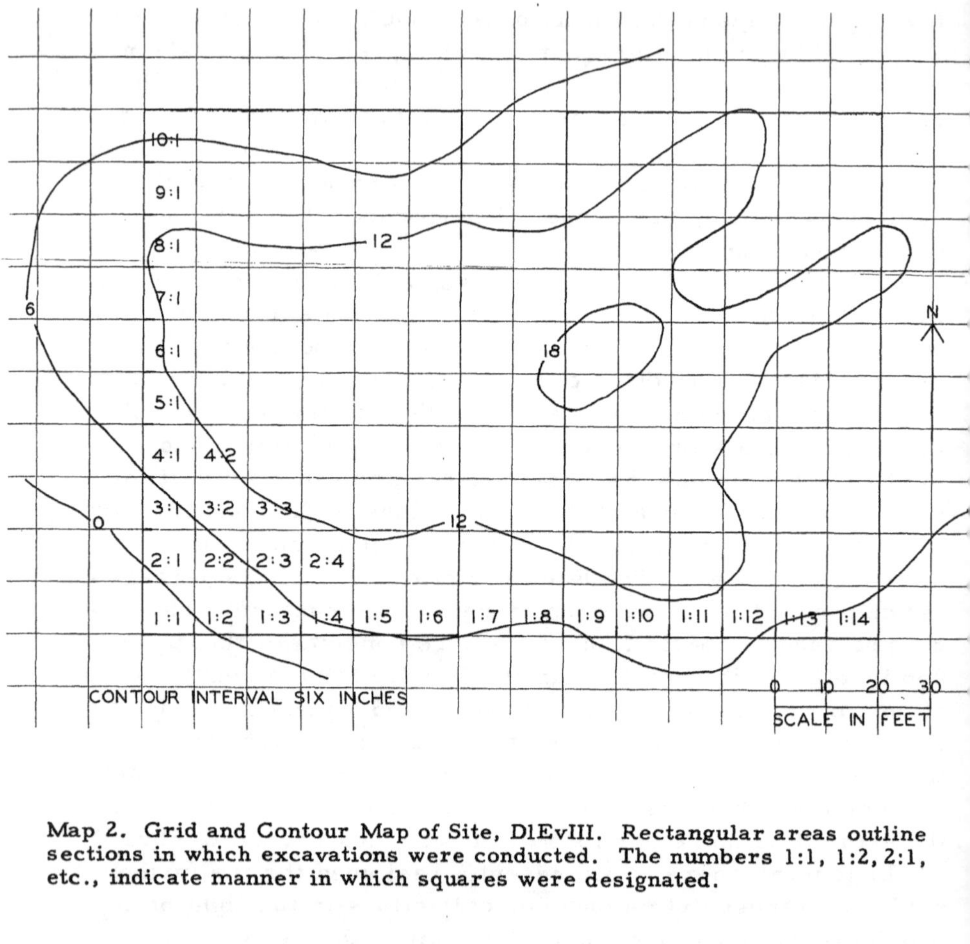

Map 2. Grid and Contour Map of Site, DlEvIII. Rectangular areas outline sections in which excavations were conducted. The numbers 1:1, 1:2, 2:1, etc., indicate manner in which squares were designated.

APPENDIX I

TRAIT LIST OF SITES IN NORTHEASTERN OKLAHOMA

Trait List, D1EvIII	Zone A	Zone B	Zone C	Zone D
Projectile point, Type A1	..	1	..	2
Straight base	..	1	..	..
Convex base	..	..	..	2
Alternate bevel on blade	..	1	..	..
Projectile point, Type A2	..	3	..	2
Straight base	..	..	..	2
Convex base	..	1	..	..
Concave base	..	1	..	..
Straight-sided blade	..	1	..	..
Convex-sided blade	..	1	..	1
Recurved blade	..	1	..	1
Horizontal shoulder	..	2	..	1
Obtuse shoulder	..	1	..	1
Stem ground smooth	..	1	..	..
Projectile point, Type A3	..	1	..	..
Concave base	..	1	..	..
Convex-sided blade	..	1	..	..
Projectile point, Type B1	..	4	1	6
Straight base	..	..	1	2
Convex base	..	4	..	3
Concave base	..	..	..	1
Straight-sided blade	..	..	1	1
Convex-sided blade	..	4	..	2
Recurved blade	..	..	..	1
Projectile point, Type B2	..	3	1	34
Straight base	..	2	..	15
Convex base	..	1	1	14
Concave base	..	..	..	2
Straight-sided blade	..	..	..	5
Convex-sided blade	..	3	..	17
Recurved blade	..	..	..	1
Biconcave blade	..	..	..	2
Coarse serrations on blade . . .	..	1	..	..
Base and/or stem ground	..	3	..	..
Projectile point, Type B3	..	..	..	3
Straight base	..	..	..	2
Convex base	..	..	..	1
Convex-sided blade	..	..	..	2
Projectile point, Type C	..	1	..	..
Projectile point, Type E1	2	24	6	9
Straight base	2	15	2	7
Convex base	..	4	1	2
Concave base	..	5	3	..

Trait List, DlEvIII	Zone A	Zone B	Zone C	Zone D
Projectile point, Type El (cont.)				
Straight-sided blade	..	4	4	2
Convex-sided blade	..	11	1	6
Coarse serrations on blade . . .	..	1	1	..
Base and /or stem ground	..	10	2	3
Horizontal shoulder	..	10	2	4
Barbed shoulder	..	..	2	4
Obtuse shoulder	1	11	2	1
Projectile point, Type E2	..	2	1	11
Straight base	..	1	..	7
Convex base	..	..	1	4
Concave base	..	1	..	..
Straight-sided blade	..	..	1	4
Convex-sided blade	..	1	..	5
Base and/or stem ground	..	1	1	..
Horizontal shoulder	..	2	..	5
Barbed shoulder	..	..	..	5
Obtuse shoulder	..	..	1	..
Projectile point, Type H	..	..	3	1
Projectile point, deviant forms	..	1	..	3
Alternate bevel on blade	..	1	..	..
Bunt				
Sharp, rounded edge	..	1	..	1
Blunted, rounded edge	..	1	..	..
Drill				
Gradual, irregular expansion to base.	..	..	..	1
Distinct, round-outline base . . .	..	1	..	..
T-shaped form	..	1	..	..
Knives				
Rounded base	2	9	3	24
Distinct base	1	5	1	6
Core knives	4	14	2	19
Cores				
Rough, thick cores	..	2	2	18
Flat, irregular cores	1	18	7	44
Flat, ovate/pointed cores	1	4	4	10
Stemmed scraper	..	2	..	..
Side scraper	..	1	1	1
Scraper, Type B2	..	1	2	1
Scraper, Type B3	..	1	..	..
Scraper, Type Cl	..	5	..	2
Scraper, Type G	1	4	1	1

Trait List, D1EvIII	Zone A	Zone B	Zone C	Zone D
Choppers	..	6	5	15
Ground and polished forms				
Concave-faced abrader	..	7	..	3
Anvil	..	1	..	
Hammerstone	..	..	..	1
Small grinding stone	..	7	..	4
Large grinding stone	..	1 (?)	..	5
Full-grooved axe	..	1	..	..
Small mortar	..	2	..	..
Mortar or metate fragment . . .	..	..	..	1

Trait List, D1CaI	Level 1 0 - 4 inches	Level 2 4 - 8 inches	Level 3 8 - 12 inches	Level 4 12 - 16 inches	Level 5 16 - 20 inches	Level 6 20 - 24 inches
Projectile point, Type A1	7	9	5	5	4	4
Straight base	1	3	2	3	2	1
Convex base	5	3	1	1	1	2
Concave base	..	1	2	..	1	..
Base straight fracture .	1	1	..	..	..	..
Straight-sided blade . .	3	2	3	4	..	1
Convex-sided blade . .	2	2	..	..	3	2
Horizontal shoulder . .	4	6	3	2	3	3
Barbed shoulder	1	..	..	..	..	..
Obtuse shoulder	2	2	2	3	1	1
Projectile point, Type A2	7	10	7	7	6	4
Straight base	3	2	1	1	1	..
Convex base	4	7	2	5	5	4
Concave base	..	..	1	1	..	..
Base straight fracture .	..	..	2	..	..	..
Pointed base	..	..	1	..	..	..
Straight-sided blade . .	..	3	3	3	1	1
Convex-sided blade . .	4	2	1	2	5	3
Convexo-concave blade.	..	2	1	..	..	..
Projectile point, Type A3	1	2	3	1	1	..
Straight base	..	1	3	..	..	..
Convex base	1	1	..	..	1	..
Concave base	..	..	..	1	..	..
Straight-sided blade . .	1	1	1	1	..	..
Convex-sided blade . .	..	..	1	..	1	..
Projectile point, Type B1	6	9	11	13	3	..
Straight base	1	2	3	4	1	..
Convex base	5	6	8	7	1	..
Concave base	..	1	..	2	1	..
Convex-sided blade . .	3	5	8	6	2	..
Recurved blade	..	1	..	..	..	..
Projectile point, Type B2	8	7	10	5	2	2
Straight base	2	1	..	..	2	1
Convex base	5	5	10	5	..	1
Concave base	1	1	..	..	..	..
Straight-sided blade . .	1	..	..	1	..	..
Convex-sided blade . .	6	7	9	3	2	1
Convexo-concave blade.	..	..	..	1	..	1
Projectile point, Type B3	..	1	1	2	1	1
Straight base	..	1	..	..	..	1
Convex base	..	..	1	2	1	..
Convex-sided blade . .	..	1	1	1	1	1
Projectile point, Type C	4	4	5	4	2	..
Straight base	2	1	5	1	2	..

Trait List, D1CaI (cont.)	Level 1 0 - 4 inches	Level 2 4 - 8 inches	Level 3 8 - 12 inches	Level 4 12 - 16 inches	Level 5 16 - 20 inches	Level 6 20 - 23 inches
Projectile point, Type C (continued)						
Convex base	2	3	..	3	..	..
Horizontal shoulder . .	..	1	..	2	1	..
Obtuse shoulder	4	2	5	2	1	..
Projectile point, Type E1	7	7	7	6	10	1
Straight base	2	2	6	5	7	1
Convex base (slightly) .	4	3	..	..	2	..
Concave base	1	1	..	1	1	..
Straight-sided blade . .	..	..	3	1	4	..
Convex-sided blade . .	..	..	2	3	2	1
Concave-sided blade . .	..	..	..	..	1	..
Horizontal shoulder . .	1	2	2	3	1	1
Barbed shoulder	..	1	4	1	4	..
Obtuse shoulder	5	2	..	1	2	..
Projectile point, Type E2	4	6	3	3	6	2
Straight base	2	3	2	1	4	1
Convex base	1	3	1	2	2	1
Concave base	1	..	..	..	..	..
Straight-sided blade . .	2	1	..	2	4	1
Convex-sided blade . .	2	1	1	1	2	1
Horizontal shoulder . .	1	2	..	..	4	..
Barbed shoulder	3	..	1	3	1	..
Obtuse shoulder	..	2	2	..	1	1
Projectile point, Type G						
Small, unnotched	5	8	1	..	..	..
Small, narrow, corner-notched	7	5	4	2	1	..
Small, broad, corner-notched	1	3	..	..	..	..
Projectile point, Type H	..	1	..	..	..	..
Projectile point, unclassified	3	1	1	4	1	1
Bunt						
Sharp, rounded end . . .	..	1	..	..	1	..
Drill						
Gradual, irregular expansion to base . . .	..	1	1	..	..	..
Distinct, roughly round outline base	3	2	..	..	..	..
Modified projectile-point form	..	1	2	..	2	..

Trait List, D1CaI (cont.)	Level 1 0 - 4 inches	Level 2 4 - 8 inches	Level 3 8 - 12 inches	Level 4 12 - 16 inches	Level 5 16 - 20 inches	Level 6 20 - 24 inches
Knives						
Large knives, over 80 mm.	2	2	5	3	2	1
Ovate	1	2	2	2	1	..
Ovate-acuminate . .	..	..	1	1	..	..
Distinct base	..	..	2	..	1	1
Rhombic; alternate bevel	1	..	..	..	..	..
Medium sized knives, 50 - 80 mm.	3	1	3	4	..	..
Ovate	..	1	..	1	..	..
Ovate-acuminate . .	1	..	..	3	..	..
Distinct base	1	..	1	..	..	..
Asymmetrical	1	..	2	..	..	..
Small knives, below 50 mm.	..	2	..	1	..	..
Ovate	..	1	..	1	..	..
Ovate-acuminate . .	..	1	..	..	..	..
Knife basal fragments						
Rounded base	3	3	6	14	1	1
Distinct base	4	1	2	2	1	..
Stemmed knives . . .						1
Core knives	3	1	3	3	1	
Cores	5	6	5	3	2	2
Stemmed scraper . . .	..	4	..	2	3	..
Scraper, Type A	1	1	1	2	..	..
Scraper, Type C	3	3	1	1	..	..
Scraper, Type F	1	1	..	..	..	..
Scraper, unclassified .	2	..	..	..	..	..
Chipped axe, double-bitted	..	..	1	..	..	..
Ground and polished stone						
Mano	3	9	10	6	3	..
Irregular outline . .	2	1	6	1	2	..
Finished outline . . .	1	8	3	5	1	..
Single grinding face .	1	2	2	1	1	..
Two grinding faces .	2	7	8	5	2	..
Hammerstone	..	..	..	1	..	..
Crude stone bowl . .	..	1	..	..	..	..
Bone and shell						
Shell scraper	..	..	1	..	..	..
Bone awl, splinter type	..	..	..	1	..	..

Trait List, DlMcVII	Level 1 0 - 4 inches	Level 2 4 - 8 inches	Level 3 8 - 12 inches	Level 4 12 - 16 inches	Level 5 16 - 20 inches	Level 6 20 - 24 inches
Projectile point, Type A1	7	7	11	2	2	..
Straight base	1	4	3	2	1	..
Convex base	3	2	7	..	..	..
Concave base	..	1	1	..	..	..
Base straight fracture .	2	..	..	..	1	..
Pointed base	1	..	..	..	..	..
Straight-sided blade . .	3	2	3	..	..	..
Convex-sided blade . . .	2	2	5	1	1	..
Convexo-concave blade .	1	..	1	1	1	..
Horizontal shoulder . .	2	3	4	2	..	..
Barbed shoulder	3	2	2	..	..	..
Obtuse shoulder	2	2	5	..	2	..
Projectile point, Type A2	13	15	8	4	3	..
Straight base	5	2	..	1	1	..
Convex base	7	10	5	2	2	..
Concave base	..	1	..	1	..	..
Base straight fracture .	1	2	3	..	..	..
Straight-sided blade . .	4	5	2	2	2	..
Convex-sided blade . . .	7	7	6	1	1	..
Convexo-concave blade .	..	..	..	1	..	..
Projectile point, Type A3	3	2	1	3	1	..
Straight base	..	1	..	1	..	..
Convex base	3	1	1	1	..	..
Base straight fracture .	..	..	..	1	1	..
Straight-sided blade . .	2	1	1	1	..	..
Convex-sided blade . . .	..	1	..	1	1	..
Projectile point, Type B1	24	31	17	20	8	1
Straight base	4	9	5	4	2	1
Convex base	16	13	9	16	4	..
Concave base	3	9	2	..	2	..
Straight-sided blade . .	4	6	2	4	1	1
Convex-sided blade . . .	10	11	13	10	6	..
Convexo-concave blade .	..	1	..	..	..	..
Projectile point, Type B2	30	26	13	8	3	1
Straight base	10	8	4	..	1	1
Convex base	15	13	8	4	1	..
Concave base	3	2	..	2	..	..
Straight-sided blade . .	1	2	2	2	1	..
Convex-sided blade . . .	19	16	9	4	1	..
Projectile point, Type B3	5	4	1	6	..	..
Straight base	..	1	..	2	..	..
Convex base	3	2	1	2	..	..
Concave base	2	1	..	2	..	..

Trait List, D1McVII (cont.)	Level 1 0 - 4 inches	Level 2 4 - 8 inches	Level 3 8 - 12 inches	Level 4 12 - 16 inches	Level 5 16 - 20 inches	Level 6 20 - 24 inches
Projectile point, Type B3 (continued)						
Straight-sided blade . .	..	2	1	..	..	..
Convex-sided blade . . .	4	2	..	4	..	..
Convexo-concave blade .	..	..	..	1	..	..
Projectile point, Type C	6	6	2	3	2	..
Straight base	3	3	2	2	1	..
Convex base	2	2	..	1	1	..
Concave base	1	1	..	..	..	..
Horizontal shoulder . .	..	1	..	..	..	..
Barbed shoulder	1	..	..	..	..	..
Obtuse shoulder	4	3	1	3	2	..
Projectile point, Type E1	4	4	7	5	2	..
Straight base	3	3	3	5	2	..
Convex base	1	1	4	..	..	..
Straight-sided blade . .	..	2	3	..	..	..
Convex-sided blade . . .	3	..	4	4	2	..
Horizontal shoulder . .	2	1	..	..	..	..
Barbed shoulder	..	2	3	3	1	..
Obtuse shoulder	2	..	2	2	1	..
Projectile point, Type E2	5	2	7	1	2	2
Straight base	4	1	6	1	..	1
Convex base	1	..	..	..	1	..
Concave base	..	..	1	..	1	1
Straight-sided blade . .	4	..	4	1	1	1
Convex-sided blade . . .	1	..	1	..	1	..
Horizontal shoulder . .	2	2	2	1	..	..
Barbed shoulder	2	..	3	..	1	..
Obtuse shoulder	1	..	1	..	..	1
Projectile point, Type G						
Small, unnotched	7	4	1	..	..	..
Small, narrow, corner-notched	15	13	2	4	..	..
Small, broad, corner-notched	16	5	3	..	8	..
Projectile point, Type H	2	..	1	3	2	1
Projectile point, Plainview	..	..	..	1	1	..
Projectile point, unclassified	1	1	1	1	1	..
Bunt						
Sharp, rounded end . . .	..	..	2	1	1	..
Drill						
Gradual, irregular expansion to base	1	3	1	3	1	..

Trait List, D1McVII (cont.)	Level 1 0 - 4 inches	Level 2 4 - 8 inches	Level 3 8 - 12 inches	Level 4 12 - 16 inches	Level 5 16 - 20 inches	Level 6 20 - 24 inches
Drill (cont.)						
Distinct, roughly rounded base	..	2	..	..	..	..
T-shaped form	..		1	1	..	..
Elongated base form .	..	2	1	1	..	..
Modified projectile point	..	2	..	..	..	..
Knives						
Large knives, over 80 mm.	1	..	..	1	..	..
Ovate	1	..	..	1	..	..
Medium sized knives, 50-80 mm.	3	4	3	..	1	..
Ovate	1	1	..	..	..	..
Ovate-acuminate . . .	2	2	3	..	..	..
Distinct base	..	1	..	..	1	..
Small knives, below 50 mm.	1	1	1	1	..	..
Ovate-acuminate . . .	1	1	1	1	..	..
Knife fragments (basal)						
Rounded base	7	11	9	9	3	..
Distinct base	1	2	7	1	6	..
Core knives	10	3	5	5	4	1
Cores	16	31	14	11	3	..
Stemmed scraper . . .	..	5	1	..	..	..
Side scraper	..	2	..	..	1	..
Scraper, Type A	1	..	..	1	..	..
Scraper, Type B	..	..	1	..	..	..
Scraper, Type C	2	3	2	1	..	1
Scraper, Type D	..	1	..	..	1	..
Scraper, Type E	3	3	1	..	1	..
Concave-edge scraper .	..	..	1	..	..	..
Chipped axe, double-bitted	1	..	..	..	..	..
Chipped implements, ground edge	..	1	..	..	..	6
Chopper.	..	..	2	..	1	..

Trait List, D1McVII (cont.)	Level 1 0 - 4 inches	Level 2 4 - 8 inches	Level 3 8 - 12 inches	Level 4 12 - 16 inches	Level 5 16 - 20 inches	Level 6 20 - 24 inches
Ground and polished stone						
Atlatl weight	..	..	1	..	..	..
Manos	20	25	23	9	1	2
Irregular outline . . .	12	15	17	7	..	1
Finished outline	8	10	5	2	1	1
Single grinding face . .	8	4	6	..	..	..
Two grinding faces . .	10	21	17	9	1	2
Abrader, concave face .	..	1	6	1	1	..
Abrader, grooved . . .	1	..	..	..	..	..
Hammerstone	..	..	1	1	..	..
Anvil	1	1	2	..	1	..
Bone						
Deer ulna flaking tool . .	..	1	..	..	1	..
Bone awl, splinter, completely smoothed . . .	..	1	2	..	..	..
Bone awl, splinter, only tip smoothed	..	..	..	1	..	..

APPENDIX II

FURTHER ANALYSIS OF PROJECTILE POINTS FROM PRECERAMIC SITES, DELAWARE COUNTY, OKLAHOMA

In the descriptive sections the projectile points were considered in terms of a series of specific types shown in diagrammatic form in Figure 14. The sketches tend to accentuate the differences in the forms, since actually there is found a marked transition from one to another. Types A1, A2, and A3, for example, form a triad that in all probability is present in most large series of points having a contracting stem. Types B1, B2, and B3 similarly merge gradually from one variety to another. Since such groups of types suggest variants on a single continuum, they raise the question as to whether they should be split as they are into separate types, or whether it would be better to group them into a single category. There seem to be several advantages in the finer breakdown, recognizing them as distinct forms. A classification of the separate forms provides an index of the amount of variation in form of the projectile points of a given component. The dispersion or concentration indicated by the finer subdivision may well be a cultural feature. Furthermore, the variations in form are noted to have a direct effect on the size and proportions of the points. Since the analysis of size may be a field in which significant contributions can be made to the study of a given culture, it is necessary to segregate the specific forms in order to make possible the tabulation of comparable measurements.

Types A1 through A3 correspond closely to a type named Gary Stemmed by Alex D. Krieger (Newell and Krieger, 1949: 164-66). Krieger, however, includes several forms with a parallel-sided stem (Figure 57 G, I, L) which would be excluded from the more rigid form categories employed in this paper. Similarly, Krieger's Ellis Stemmed (Newell and Krieger, pp. 166-67) corresponds to Type B1. It is evident that the relationships of these types and the significance of the distribution of the projectile-point forms comprise one of the important current archaeological problems. The following discussion of measurement indicates a potential technique that may be of use in comparative studies of projectile-point types.

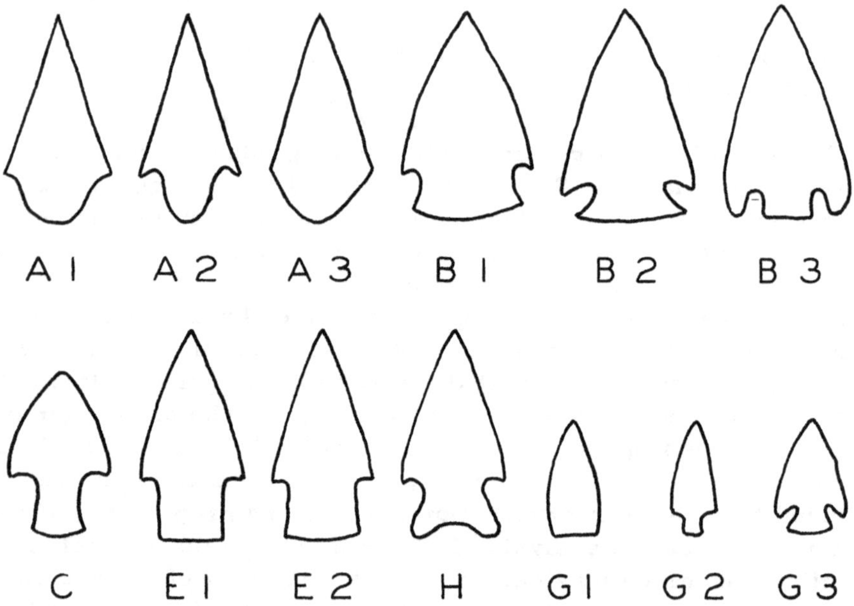

Fig. 14. Projectile Point Types of Preceramic Sites in Northeastern Oklahoma.

The mean dimensions of the projectile points were noted in the preceding pages in connection with the description of implements found in the various sites. At that point no further discussion was given of the implications of these measurements since the methodology and significance of this phase of the descriptive procedure were not elaborated. In a preliminary statement, Baerreis and Hornseth (1948) indicated a procedure whereby through an analysis of measurement it would be possible to discover whether a given complex has culturally determined standards of absolute size, fixed proportions of the dimensions of the points, or a definite relation in size between component parts of the point. The suggested procedure involved no novel techniques but rather the simple application of standard statistical techniques to conventional measurements. The analysis was directed toward a better understanding of what the measurements reveal, specifically in terms of cultural data. By a comparison of the statistics of a series of points of Type A from two distinct cultural complexes in southern and eastern Oklahoma, it was found that the two complexes had differing standards of absolute size and also differences in some correlations between component parts of the point. These standards appear to have governed the worker as an ideal type to which his products conformed.

The preliminary report cited above served to indicate that two different cultural units had sizes and proportions that differed in a statistically significant quantity in the projectile points of similar form common to both cultures. In the absence of comparative material the study could not determine whether the differences were simply a statistical artifact or whether there were real cultural standards that would consistently characterize the sites of a given culture. Specifically, would other sites of the same culture yield projectile points of the same shape that had similar mean dimensions? Further measurements were made to give an answer to this problem. Projectile points of Type A from two additional Fourche Maline Focus sites (LfSaI and LfMaI) in LeFlore County, Oklahoma, were studied in order to obtain measurements that could be compared with those from LfHeII already presented in the preliminary report. The mean dimensions of projectile points of Type A1 from the three sites are presented in Table XII below. The close correspondence of the means of a single culture complex from the three sites leaves little room to doubt the

TABLE XII

Mean Dimensions (in mm.) of Projectile Points of Type A1 from Fourche Maline Focus Sites in LeFlore County, Oklahoma

Site:	LfHeII	LfSaI	LfMaI
Number in sample	76	86	110
Mean length	52.0	52.9	52.9
Mean width	27.6	27.7	29.2
Mean stem length	17.3	16.4	17.9

reality of the existence of cultural standards governing the size of the projectile points. The distribution of projectile points of the shape of Type A in many presumably unrelated cultural complexes had posed the problem of whether or not these points could be used to determine specific cultural affiliations. The study of size and proportions, however, promises to constitute an aspect of analysis which may be useful in determining cultural relationships through artifact types that would otherwise lack diagnostic features.

Table XIII gives the mean dimensions of projectile points of Types A1, A2, and A3 for sites D1EvIII, D1CaI, and D1McVII with the table divided to show the differences that are to be found in the three temporal phases described for the preceramic period. Two things may be noted in this table. First, the preceramic sites in northeastern Oklahoma show a definite trend of decreasing size in maximum length and width from the earliest periods to the latest. Second, all of the means of length and width from Delaware County preceramic sites exceed in a significant quantity the means of points of the same type in sites of Bryan and LeFlore counties, which have a different cultural affiliation. (The means for points of Type A1 for Fourche Maline Focus sites in LeFlore County are presented in Table XII.) The preliminary report of Baerreis and Hornseth (1948) indicated that a second culture isolated in Bryan County had Type A1 points with a mean length of 43.5 mm., a mean width of 22.7 mm., and a mean stem length of 15.3 mm. Different cultural standards in size would therefore appear to have been held by the manufacturers of projectile points in the different cultural complexes considered.

TABLE XIII

Mean Dimensions (in mm.) of Projectile Points of Types A1-3 for Sites DlEvIII, DlCaI, and DlMcVII in Delaware County, Northeastern Oklahoma

	DlEvIII	Levels 4-6		Levels 1-3	
		DlCaI	DlMcVII	DlCaI	DlMcVII
Type A1					
Mean length	(N1) 84.0	(N6) 76.7	....	(N6) 63.2	(N13) 66.5
Mean width	(N3) 36.7	(N12) 34.1	(N6) 32.8	(N23) 32.9	(N36) 32.8
Mean stem length	(N3) 16.3	(N16) 20.7	(N6) 19.3	(N27) 19.8	(N40) 19.4
Type A2					
Mean length	(N2) 86.5	(N2) 69.0	(N2) 72.0	(N2) 59.0	(N5) 60.6
Mean width	(N4) 41.0	(N13) 36.4	(N5) 33.4	(N15) 33.1	(N22) 35.3
Mean stem length	(N3) 19.0	(N13) 19.5	(N6) 19.7	(N25) 20.0	(N19) 18.5
Type A3					
Mean length	....	(N2) 70.5	....	(N3) 67.0	(N1) 66.0
Mean width	(N1) 30.0	(N2) 31.0	(N4) 31.3	(N4) 27.5	(N4) 24.7
Mean stem length	(N1) 21.0	(N2) 20.0	(N4) 18.7	(N4) 19.5	(N4) 18.3

It is to be noted in Table XIII that the same trends of decreasing size are found in all of the Type A points – Types A2 and A3 as well as Type A1. There are, however, differences in some aspects, such as mean width, which are no doubt directly due to differences in form. Type A3, the form lacking a shoulder area, is markedly narrower than the other two types. In regard to the trend of decreasing size, LfHeII, LfSaI, and LfMaI, as well as BrJaI, are considered to represent a later time period than the preceramic components in Delaware County. The LeFlore County sites (LfHeII, LfSaI, and LfMaI), are pottery-bearing components classified in the Fourche Maline Focus, a local and probably late survival of the Archaic of the Southeast. BrJaI, a site having means that are even smaller than the Fourche Maline Focus sites, was for the most part a ceramic midden though it appears to be transitional to a ceramic culture in this region, the Bryan Focus. It is therefore possible to postulate that, in general, eastern Oklahoma at this period of occupation was undergoing a decrease in size of projectile points. Confirmatory evidence is needed on this point, but it may indicate the possibility of placing a culture in a rough time period according to the mean dimensions of the projectile points. The standards thus far demonstrated are based on only a few projectile point types, and it is necessary to determine precisely what happened in other types.

For the preceramic complex the number of projectile points of each type in a given site and period is too small for further statistical analysis. In order to make such an analysis, all points of a given type from the three sites, DlEvIII, DlCaI, and DlMcVII, have been combined into a single series and the statistics presented in Table XIV. A comparison of the mean, variance, and coefficient of variation of the various types in this table indicates significant differences among them. On this basis it is evident that we are not justified in grouping together Types A1, A2, and A3. In all three types, the correlation between length and width, despite the small sample, is sufficiently large to indicate that the correlation differs significantly from zero; that is, it indicates a real degree of association between the two variables. This is also true of the correlation between width and stem length in Types A1 and A2. In the remaining correlations the value of $\underline{r}$ is not sufficiently large, considering the size of the sample, to indicate a significant correlation. The reason for the computation, however, was to

TABLE XIV

Selected Statistics of Projectile Points of Types A1, A2, and A3 for Sites DlEvIII, DlCaI, and DlMcVII

Statistics	Type A1	Type A2	Type A3
Mean length in mm.	(N26) 67.3	(N13) 67.4	(N6) 68.0
Variance in length	141.04	194.47	146.0
Coefficient of Variation	26	21	18
Mean width in mm.	(N79) 33.2	(N56) 35.3	(N16) 28.5
Variance in width	21.34	27.25	21.12
Coefficient of Variation	14	15	16
Mean stem length in mm.	(N90) 19.6	(N57) 19.5	(N16) 19.3
Variance in stem length	11.12	5.96	31.94
Coefficient of Variation	17	31	29
Correlation between			
length and width	(N26) .486	(N12) .689	(N6) .726
length and stem length	(N26) .318	(N13) .456	(N6) .812
width and stem length	(N79) .402	(N56) .459	(N16) .207
body length and stem length	(N26) .212	(N13) .351	(N6) .396

determine specifically if the culture had fixed standards of proportions that could be compared or contrasted with the standards used in other cultural complexes. Comparative material was provided in the study of Baerreis and Hornseth (1948) from which we may abstract data provided for sites BrJaI and LfHeII regarding points of Type A1 made of chert, the same material used in northeastern Oklahoma. This information is given in Table XV.

TABLE XV

Correlations Between Component Parts of Projectile Points of Type A1 for Sites in Eastern Oklahoma

	Preceramic Sites NE Oklahoma	BrJaI	LfHeII
Correlation between			
length and width	(N26) .486	(N36) .354	(N17) .367
length and stem length	(N26) .643	(N36) .751	(N17) .293
width and stem length	(N79) .402	(N36) .335	(N17) .069
body length and stem length	(N26) .516	(N36) .575	(N17) .077

The correlations indicate that different standards are present in the different cultural complexes, though the preceramic sites and BrJaI show a general similarity. Such correlations, however, are important in providing an analysis of features that are considered in only general terms in the form classification. These, together with the analysis of size, provide a means of comparing projectile points of similar shape found in different cultural complexes to determine the degree of likeness or unlikeness. In the present stage of research on this particular problem, we can do little more than establish the standards of various cultural complexes. As more comparative data become available, the utility of such a statistical approach as a tool should increase in value.

The mean dimensions of the remaining projectile-point types of the preceramic components in northeastern Oklahoma are tabulated in Table XVI. For the most part, the numbers available do not warrant additional statistical analysis. As suggested above, however, the significance of the measurements should increase with additional research.

TABLE XVI

Mean Dimensions (in mm.) of Projectile Points from Preceramic Sites in Delaware County

Types	DlEvIII	DlCaI	DlMcVII
Type B1			
Mean length	66.0 (N1)	56.0 (N16)	51.5 (N19)
Mean width	34.3 (N7)	34.4 (N35)	33.0 (N35)
Mean stem length	16.3 (N11)	14.4 (N37)	14.6 (N70)
Type B2			
Mean length	66.3 (N11)	53.5 (N13)	51.0 (N12)
Mean width	39.3 (N25)	39.0 (N26)	35.8 (N35)
Mean stem length	13.9 (N34)	13.5 (N31)	12.9 (N41)
Type B3			
Mean length	56.0 (N1)	53.0 (N1)	60.5 (N2)
Mean width	39.0 (N1)	49.0 (N2)	38.2 (N4)
Mean stem length	13.0 (N3)	13.8 (N6)	12.0 (N5)
Type C			
Mean length	....	49.7 (N7)	49.5 (N2)
Mean width	....	25.9 (N16)	24.2 (N12)
Mean stem length	14.0 (N1)	14.2 (N17)	14.7 (N14)
Type E1			
Mean length	72.7 (N12)	72.5 (N8)	61.6 (N5)
Mean width	38.5 (N27)	34.5 (N27)	37.6 (N14)
Mean stem length	17.8 (N40)	17.6 (N33)	16.8 (N20)
Type E2			
Mean length	61.0 (N4)	61.6 (N12)	70.6 (N3)
Mean width	38.0 (N9)	36.8 (N22)	37.4 (N13)
Mean stem length	16.1 (N13)	16.6 (N23)	16.3 (N14)
Type H			
Mean length	51.3 (N3)	....	54.5 (N2)
Mean width	25.0 (N4)	13.0 (N1)	27.2 (N4)
Mean stem length	16.6 (N3)	18.0 (N1)	8.5 (N4)
Type G1			
Mean length	....	31.1 (N10)	38.2 (N5)
Mean width	....	15.2 (N15)	18.3 (N11)
Type G2			
Mean length	....	26.5 (N9)	23.9 (N12)
Mean width	....	11.0 (N19)	11.8 (N23)
Type C3			
Mean length	....	31.0 (N1)	35.6 (N10)
Mean width	....	17.0 (N1)	21.6 (N21)

BIBLIOGRAPHY

Amsden, Charles A.
1937 The Lake Mohave Artifacts. In: The Archeology of Pleistocene Lake Mohave, a Symposium. Southwest Mus. Papers, No. 11.

Baerreis, David A.
1939 Two New Cultures in Delaware County, Oklahoma. In: The Oklahoma Prehistorian, II, No. 1: 2-5.
1940 The Neosho Focus. Soc. Amer. Archaeol. Notebook, pp. 108-9. (Mimeographed.)
1947 Spiro Focus Basketry. Mus. Univ. Oklahoma. Information Ser., Circular II: 1-12.

Baerreis, David A., and R. A. Hornseth
1948 Measurement in Projectile Point Description: A Preliminary Statement. News Letter, Plains Archeolog. Conf. I, No. 4: 13-15.

Bushnell, David I., Jr.
1905 Fragmentary Textiles from Ozark Caves. Journ. Washington Acad. Sci., V: 318-23.

Carter, George F.
1945 Plant Geography and Culture History in the American Southwest. Viking Fund Publ. Anthropol., No. 5.

Claflin, William H.
1931 The Stalling's Island Mound, Columbia County, Georgia. Papers Peabody Mus. Amer. Archaeol. and Ethnol., XIV, No. 1.

Cosgrove, C. B.
1947 Caves of the Upper Gila and Hueco Areas in New Mexico and Texas. Papers Peabody Mus. Amer. Archaeol. and Ethnol., XXIV, No. 2.

Dellinger, S. C.
1936 Baby Cradles of the Ozark Bluff Dwellers. Amer. Antiq., I, No. 3: 197-214.

Dellinger, S. C., and S. D. Dickinson
1942 Pottery from the Ozark Bluff Shelters. Ibid., VII, No. 3: 276-90.

Eichenberger, J. Allen
1944 Investigations of the Marion-Ralls Archaeological Society in Northeast Missouri. The Missouri Archaeologist, No. 19: 1-68.

Ford, J. A., and G. I. Quimby
1945 The Tchefuncte Culture, and Early Occupation of the Lower Mississippi Valley. Mem. Soc. Amer. Archaeol., Suppl. to Amer. Antiq., X, No. 3.

Ford, J. A., and G. R. Willey
1940 Crooks Site, a Marksville Period Burial Mound in La Salle Parish, Louisiana. Louisiana Dept. Conserv., Anthropol. Study, No. 3.

Fowke, Gerard
1922 Archeological Investigations. Bur. Amer. Ethnol. Bull., 76.

Funkhouser, W. D., and W. S. Webb
1929 The So-Called "Ash Caves" in Lee County, Kentucky. Univ. Kentucky Repts. Archaeol. and Anthropol., 1, No. 2.

Gilmore, Melvin R.
1930 Vegetal Remains of the Ozark Bluff-Dweller Culture. Papers Mich. Acad., XIV: 83-102.

Gladwin, H. S., E. W. Haury, E. B. Sayles, and N. Gladwin
1937 Excavations at Snaketown, Material Culture. Medallion Papers, No. XXV (Gila Pueblo, Globe, Arizona).

Griffin, James B.
1946 Cultural Change and Continuity in Eastern United States Archaeology. In: Man in Northeastern North America. Papers Peabody Found. Archaeol., III.

Guernsey, S. J., and A. V. Kidder
1921 Basket-Maker Caves of Northeastern Arizona. Report on the Explorations, 1916-1917. Papers Peabody Mus. Amer. Archaeol. and Ethnol., VIII, No. 2.

Harrington, M. R.
1920 Certain Caddo Sites in Arkansas. Indian Notes and Monogr., No. 10.
1924 The Ozark Bluff-Dwellers. Amer. Anthropologist, 26, No. 1: 1-21.
1933 Gypsum Cave, Nevada. Southwest Mus. Papers, No. 8.

Haury, E. W., and E. B. Sayles
1947 An Early Pit House Village of the Mogollon Culture, Forestdale Valley, Arizona. Univ. Arizona Social Sci. Bull., No. 16. Bull., 18, No. 4.

Holmes, William H.
1903 Flint Implements and Fossil Remains from a Sulphur Spring at Afton, Indian Territory. Rept. U. S. Nat. Mus., 1901, pp. 233-52.

Jones, Volney H.
1936 The Vegetal Remains of Newt Kash Hollow Shelter. In: Rock Shelters in Menifee County, Kentucky, by W. S. Webb and W. D. Funkhouser. Univ. Kentucky Repts. in Archaeol. and Anthropol., 3, No. 4: 147-67.
1946 Review of Plant Geography and Culture History in the American Southwest, by George F. Carter. Amer. Antiq., XI, No. 4: 262-65.
1949 Maize from the Davis Site: Its Nature and Interpretation. In: The George C. Davis Site, Cherokee County, Texas, by H. Perry Newell and Alex D. Krieger. Soc. Amer. Archaeol., No. 5. Appendix.

Kelley, J. Charles
1947 The Cultural Affiliations and Chronological Position of the Clear Fork Focus. Amer. Antiq., XIII, No. 2: 97-109.

Kidder, A. V.
1938 Arrow-Heads or Dart Points. Amer. Antiq., IV, No. 2: 156-57.

Kidder, A. V., and S. J. Guernsey
1919 Archaeological Explorations in Northeastern Arizona. Bur. Amer. Ethnol., Bull., 65.

Krieger, Alex D.
1944 The Typological Concept. Amer. Antiq., IX, No. 3: 271-88.
1946 Culture Complexes and Chronology in Northern Texas. Univ. Texas Publ., No. 4640.
1947 Artifacts from the Plainview Bison Bed. In: Fossil Bison and Associated Artifacts from Plainview, Texas, by E. H. Sellards, Glen L. Evans, and Grayson E. Meade. Bull. Geol. Soc. Amer., 58: 927-54.

Lewis, Thomas M. N., and Madeline Kneberg
1947 The Archaic Horizon in Western Tennessee. Tennessee Anthropol. Papers, No. 2.

MacNeish, Richard S.
1948 The Pre-Pottery Faulkner Site of Southern Illinois. Amer. Antiq., 13: 232-43.

Martin, Paul S.
1940 The SU Site: Excavations at a Mogollon Village, Western New Mexico, 1939. Field Mus. Nat. Hist., Anthropol. Ser., XXXI, No. 1.
1943 SU Site: Excavations at a Mogollon Village, Western New Mexico, Second Season, 1941. Ibid., XXXII No. 2.

Martin, Paul S., George I. Quimby, and Donald Collier
1947 Indians Before Columbus. Chicago: Univ. Chicago Press.

Martin, Paul S., and John B. Rinaldo
1947 The SU Site: Excavations at a Mogollon Village, Western New Mexico, Third Season, 1946. Field Mus. Nat. Hist., Anthropol. Ser., XXXII, No. 3.

Morris, Earl H., and Robert F. Burgh
1941 Anasazi Basketry: Basket Maker II through Pueblo III. Carnegie Instit. Wash. Publ., 533.

Newell, H. Perry, and Alex D. Krieger
1949 The George C. Davis Site, Cherokee County, Texas. Mem. Soc. Amer. Archaeol., No. 5.

Newkumet, Phil J.
1940 Preliminary Report on Excavation of the Williams Mound, LeFlore County, Oklahoma. In: The Oklahoma Prehistorian, III, No. 2: 2-6.

Nusbaum, J. L.
1922 A Basket-Maker Cave in Kane County, Utah; with notes on the artifacts by A. V. Kidder and S. J. Guernsey. Indian Notes and Monographs, Misc. Paper, No. 29. Mus. Amer. Indian, Heye Foundation.

Peabody, Charles, and W. K. Moorehead
1904 Explorations of Jacobs Cavern, McDonald County, Missouri. Phillips Academy, Dept. Archeol., Bull., 1.

Ritchie, William A.
1944 The Pre-Iroquoian Occupations of New York State. Rochester Mus. Mem., No. 1.

Roberts, Frank H. H., Jr.
1946 Carter's Thesis in the Light of Archaeology: The Southwest. Amer. Antiq., XI, No. 4: 266-69.

Sayles, E. B.
1945 The San Simon Branch – Excavations at Cave Creek and in the San Simon Valley; 1, Material Culture. Medallion Papers, No. XXXIV (Gila Pueblo, Globe Arizona).

Sayles, E. B., and E. Antevs
1941 The Cochise Culture. Medallion Papers, No. XXIX (Gila Pueblo, Globe, Arizona).

Steward, Julian H.
1940 Native Cultures of the Intermontane (Great Basin) Area. Smithson. Misc. Coll., 100: 445-502.

Strong, W. D.
1935 An Introduction to Nebraska Archaeology. Smithson. Misc. Coll., XCIII, No. 10.

Webb, W. S., and D. I. DeJarnette
1942 Archeological Survey of the Pickwick Basin in the Adjacent Portions of the States of Alabama, Mississippi, and Tennessee. Bur. Amer. Ethnol., Bull., 129.
1948 The Flint River Site, Ma°48. Mus. Paper 23, Ala. Mus. Nat. Hist., Univ. Ala.

Webb, W. S., and W. D. Funkhouser
1936 Rock Shelters in Menifee County, Kentucky. Univ. Kentucky Repts. Anthropol. and Archaeol., 3, No. 4.

Webb, W. S., and W. G. Haag
1939 The Chiggerville Site, Site No. 1, Ohio County, Kentucky. Univ. Kentucky Repts. Anthropol. and Archaeol., 4, No. 1.
1947 Archaic Sites in McLean County, Kentucky. Ibid., 7, No. 1.

Wedel, Waldo A.
1940 Culture Sequences in the Central Great Plains. Smithson. Misc. Coll., 100; 291-352.

Weltfish, Gene
1932 Problems in the Study of Ancient and Modern Basket-Makers. Amer. Anthropol., 34, No. 1: 108-117

Willey, Gordon R.
1946 Carter's Thesis in the Light of Archaeology: The Southeast. Amer. Antiq., XI, No. 4: 265-66.

PLATE I.

Projectile Points from the Oklahoma Preceramic Components. A-E, I-L, O — site DlEvIII; F-H, M-N — site DlMcVII. A — Type A1; B — Type B1; C-E — Type B2; F-I — Type H; J — Type E1; K-L — unclassified; M-N — Plainview form; O — partially completed point.

PLATE II.

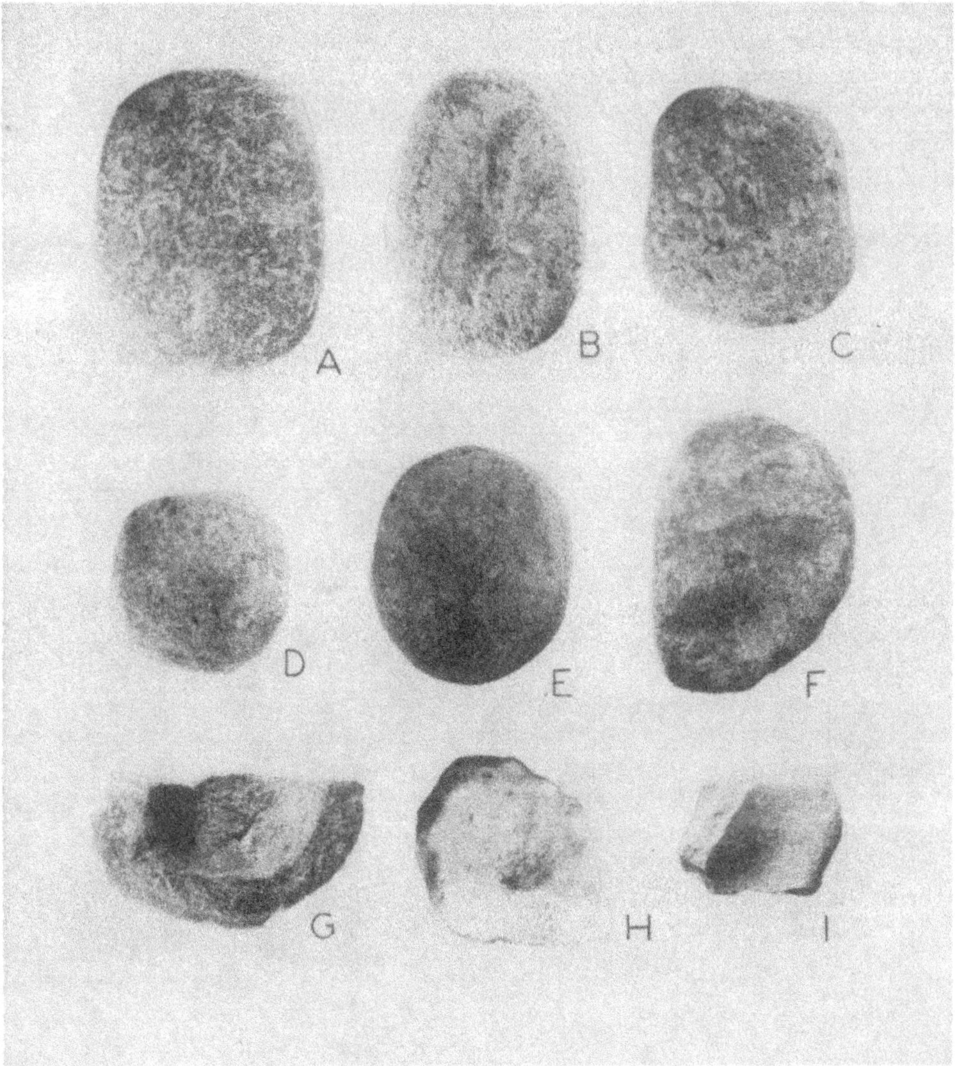

Ground Stone Implements from the Oklahoma Preceramic Components. A-D, F — site DlMcVII; E, G — site DlCaI; H-I — DlEvIII. A-D — manos; E — mano used as abrader; F — abrader; G — stone bowl; H-I — mortars.

PLATE III.

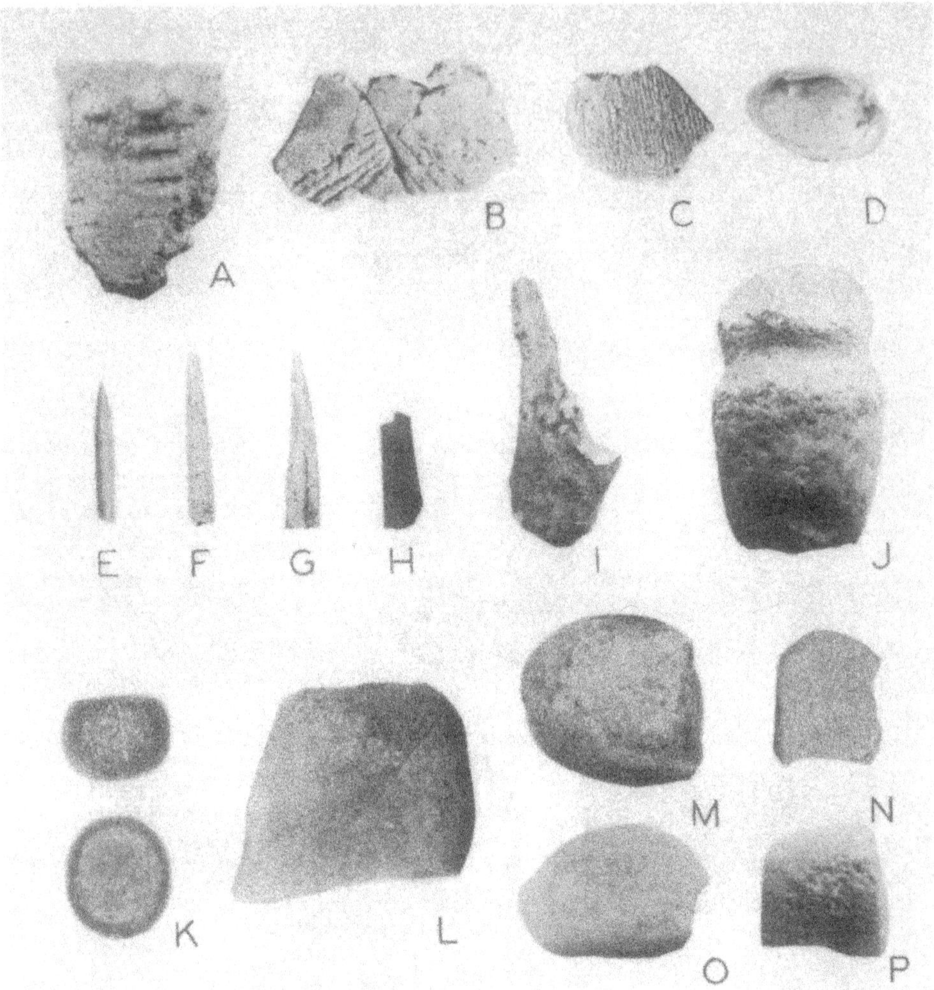

Pottery, Bone, and Stone Artifacts from the Oklahoma Sites. A-B, D-E — site DlCaI; C, F-I, K — site DlMcVII; J, L-P — site DlEvIII. A — Hopewellian type sherd; B — Neosho Punctate type sherd; C — Woodland type sherd; D — shell scraper; E-H — bone awls; I — flaking tool; J — full-grooved axe; K — boatstone; L — large grinding stone; M, O — small grinding stones; N — abrader; P — anvil.

www.ingramcontent.com/pod-product-compliance
Lightning Source LLC
LaVergne TN
LVHW050022250826
846302LV00008B/59